T0361172

FOREIGN DIRECT INVESTMENT IN KOREA

This book is dedicated to my parents Leo and Donna Bishop, my wife Kathy, my sons Robert and Stuart and my brothers Daniel and Michael.

Foreign Direct Investment in Korea

The Role of the State

DR BERNIE BISHOP
Griffith University

Routledge
Taylor & Francis Group

LONDON AND NEW YORK

First published 1997 by Ashgate Publishing

Reissued 2018 by Routledge
2 Park Square, Milton Park, Abingdon, Oxon, OX14 4RN
711 Third Avenue, New York, NY 10017, USA

Routledge is an imprint of the Taylor & Francis Group, an informa business

Publisher's Note
The publisher has gone to great lengths to ensure the quality of this reprint but points out that some imperfections in the original copies may be apparent.

Disclaimer
The publisher has made every effort to trace copyright holders and welcomes correspondence from those they have been unable to contact.

A Library of Congress record exists under LC control number: 97074451

ISBN 13: 978-1-138-31325-5 (hbk)
ISBN 13: 978-0-429-45769-2 (ebk)

Contents

List of Tables

Acknowledgments

At the outset I would like to acknowledge the inspiration help and guidance given to me by my friend and supervisor Andrew MacIntyre, who supervised the thesis upon which this book is based. Without his continuing encouragement this work may never have been completed.

I would next like to acknowledge the valuable help and insights given to me by many friends and colleagues in Korea. I would like to thank Professors Wan Soon Kim, Linsu Kim, Yoon Dae Euh, Jae Ho Yeom, Gil Sung Park and Byung Kook Kim all of Korea University who were kind enough to talk to me about the topic and arrange many interviews for me. I would also like to acknowledge the help of Professors Myong Soon Shin and Chung In Moon from Yonsei University, Professor Chung Kil Chung from Seoul National University, Professor Jee In Jang of Chungang University and Man Hak Kwon from Kyung Hee University all of whom took the time to speak to me about the issues involved in this book and provide valuable insights.

In addition I would like to thank those people in the Korean Ministry of Trade Industry and Energy and the Ministry of Finance and the Economy who were all always most helpful in answering my many questions. More generally I would like to acknowledge the cooperation and readiness of persons in the many research institutes and other government and private organisations consulted to provide information to assist with this research. In all cases there was a genuine interest in the topic and an openness to the enquires that I was making.

I would like to acknowledge the considerable degree of support from Griffith University and the Faculty of Asian and International Studies in particular. I would like to express my thanks to Robyn White and Jennilyn Mann for their assistance with the final formatting work.

I would also like to acknowledge grants by the Australia Korea Foundation, the National Korean Studies Centre and the Faculty of Asian and International Studies which facilitated the research conducted in Korea.

Finally I would like to thank my wife Kathy, sons Robert and Stuart, my parents, brothers and all other members of my extended family for their support and encouragement and the motivation to complete the task.

List of Abbreviations

APEC	Asia Pacific Economic Cooperation forum
EPB	Economic Planning Board
FKI	Federation of Korean Industries
FKTU	Federation of Korean Trade Unions
GATT	General Agreement on Tariffs and Trade
HCI	Heavy and Chemical Industry program
KCIA	Korean Central Intelligence Agency
IMF	International Monetary Fund
KDI	Korea Development Institute
KIEP	Korea Institute for International Economic Policy
KIET	Korea Institute for Economics and Technology
MCI	Ministry of Commerce and Industry
MNC	Multinational Corporation
MOF	Ministry of Finance
MTI	Ministry of Trade and Industry (successor to MCI)
OECD	Organisation for Economic Cooperation and Development
UNCTC	United Nations Centre for Transnational Corporations
US	United States of America
USITC	United States International Trade Commission

Introduction

During the 1960s and 1970s Korean policy makers adopted a highly interventionist approach to foreign investment using policy measures to channel it into those sectors of the economy where it could best assist in achieving the state's development goals. Foreign investment played a significant role as a learning agent for Korean firms in international marketing skills and as a source of technology for those Korean industries where technology could not be acquired more cost effectively. At the same time many of the adverse consequences that other countries had experienced from foreign investment were able to be avoided.

In the 1980s top policy makers sought to change policy direction to a more market oriented approach. This meant liberalising the controls over foreign investment so that it could play a greater role among alternative sources of foreign capital and also act as a competitive spur to local industries. They believed that competitive pressures would assist in restructuring industry in line with standards of international competitiveness and provide the means for local firms to upgrade their technological capabilities. The attempts to change policy were ineffective both in terms of the extent to which actual changes in policy occurred and in terms of the outcomes that resulted.

The inability of policy makers to realise their objectives to liberalise foreign investment in the 1980s appears to have been overcome to a certain extent in recent years. The Kim administration has succeeded in achieving significant deregulation of the controls over foreign investment. This is essentially what key policy makers in the early years of the Chun administration had hoped to achieve at that time.

The question that this book addresses is why there have been variations in the state's ability to achieve its policy objectives in relation to foreign investment. Policy objectives in the 1960s and 1970s were achieved as evidenced by the favourable outcomes from foreign investment. Yet in the 1980s and early 1990s the objectives that policy makers had in terms of liberalising policy were not met either in terms of actual change in policy itself or in terms of the desired outcomes of key policy makers. It has only been in recent years that foreign investment policy seems once again to be exhibiting outcomes which align with the objectives of key policy makers.

The argument in this book is that the degree to which foreign investment policy objectives were able to be achieved can be explained by

1

state capacity. The capacity of the state depends in turn upon the twin features of bureaucratic capacity and political capacity. Bureaucratic capacity refers to the extent to which the state is able to competently and cohesively formulate and implement policy. It arises out of the institutional arrangements which the state has in place in relation to a particular policy area, the stance that the political leadership and top bureaucrats within the state adopt and the degree to which the leadership is able to mobilise the bureaucracy in support of its policy objectives. The political capacity of the state refers to the state's ability to carry society along with its policy goals. In turn this depends upon the state maintaining a degree of insulation in the formulation and implementation of policy while at the same time remaining sufficiently embedded within society to ensure acceptance or at the very least compliance with policy initiatives. The state is also part of a wider international society which may impose constraints on policy makers.

The issue of the capacity of the Korean state for effective policy formulation and implementation has been widely canvassed in a branch of the political economy literature which could be broadly described as institutionalist. As Haggard and Moon (1990: 210–13) point out, this branch of the literature seeks to explain the political determinants of policy choice and effectiveness. They note that variations in institutional arrangements between the state and its society and the internal structure of policy making bodies helps to 'account for variations in policy choice and thus for economic performance' (Haggard and Moon 1990: 211). Haggard (1994: 270–1) suggests that institutionalist explanations for policy choice revolve around the bureaucratic capacity of the state, its political capacity and the policy instruments that the state is able to utilise to bring about its policy objectives.

The institutionalist literature has dealt extensively with bureaucratic and political capacity in the context of the Korean developmental state. The bureaucratic capacity of the state has been described as having arisen in part out of a long standing bureaucratic tradition (Kohli 1994; Cumings 1987) and the structuring of the bureaucratic institutions by the Park administration to take advantage of that tradition (Kim B.K. 1992; Choi 1991(a) and (b); Haggard and Moon 1990). The leadership style of Park and his political appointees has also been advanced as an explanation for the cohesiveness of the internal policy making institutions of the state (Moon and Prasad 1994: 365–7). Less attention has been paid to a third determinant of the cohesiveness within these institutions. This was the ability of the leadership to motivate and unify the bureaucracy through an appeal to development goals through what has been called a developmental ideology (Kim K.W. 1991(a); Paik 1991(a); Chung C.K. 1986).

The political capacity of the developmental state has been described as having arisen out of the formation of a development coalition between the state and big business in which the state was the dominant partner (Haggard 1988: 234; Moon 1994: 146, MacIntyre 1990: 8; Matthews and Ravenhill 1994: 72–3) and through the exclusion of other societal actors from direct input into policy processes (Choi J.J. 1989; Deyo 1987; Koo 1987; Matthews and Ravenhill 1994: 75). The corporatist arrangements that the state adopted in relation to labour and small business (Park M.K. 1987; Onis 1987) and the formal constitutional arrangements that political leaders adopted to establish supremacy of the executive over the national assembly (Moon and Prasad 1994: 362) have been advanced as explanations for the inability of societal forces to have direct input into policy yet at the same time ensuring societal compliance with the state's policy objectives. However, compliance is not a sufficient condition for high levels of performance (Kim K.H. 1993). In this respect the literature may have underestimated the role of the state's developmental ideology in carrying society along with the state's policy goals. The literature may also have underestimated the degree to which policy makers were either assisted or constrained by the international economic and political environment. This is of considerable importance in many areas of economic policy including foreign investment policy.

The decline in the state's capacity in the 1980s to cohesively formulate and implement policy and to maintain its insulation from societal actors has been less widely discussed in the institutionalist literature. A number of writers refer to the reduction in the state's political capacity by reference to the increasing political power of big business groups (Haggard and Moon 1990; Moon 1994, MacIntyre 1990, Kim E.M. 1988; Haggard 1994; Lee and Lee 1992: 16). Others refer to the state's reduced capacity arising from the greater need to take societal concerns into account following the significant steps towards democratisation which have occurred since 1987 (Evans 1992, 1995; Johnson 1994: 76–7; Haggard and Moon 1990; Shafer 1990: 137; Moon and Kim; Lee and Lee 1992: 21). Some authors have also drawn attention to the increasing constraints that policy makers have faced since the mid 1980s due to changes in the international political and economic environment (Cotton 1994).

The issue of the state's reduced bureaucratic capacity has attracted attention in relation to some particular issues. Choi (1991a; 1991b) has drawn attention to the difficulties of top policy makers in introducing economic liberalisation measures in the early 1980s due to a significant reduction in cohesiveness within the bureaucracy. In a similar vein, Rhee (1994) has examined the limitations of industrial restructuring arising out of the state's internal institutional arrangements and its relations with business groups.

It is accepted here that in order to explain the state's varying capacity to formulate and implement foreign investment policy effectively requires a consideration of both bureaucratic capacity and political capacity. However as Moon and Prasad (1994: 365–7) have argued it is necessary to look at the components of each and their interrelationship rather than adopt a highly aggregated approach to the state. It is argued here that bureaucratic capacity results from the interplay between the structuring of bureaucratic institutions, the role that the political leadership plays in relation to the bureaucracy and the ability of the leadership to motivate the bureaucracy. Similarly, a reduction in bureaucratic capacity can occur due to changed institutional arrangements in relation to a particular issue or from constraints that impede action by the leadership. Most significantly, the role that a widely accepted ideology plays in maintaining cohesiveness in the bureaucracy and the role that leadership plays in this regard needs to be emphasised. In short, as Liddell (1992), Johnson (1994) and Gourevitch (1993) have pointed out, leadership matters. But so too does the view held by policy makers within the various bureaucratic institutions of the state as to the most appropriate role for the state in a particular policy area.

It is also accepted here that the state's embedded autonomy in relation to society has been a necessary condition for effective policy making. However, embedded autonomy is its own grave digger (Evans 1995: 227; Moon and Kim: 8) because effectiveness of state policies in meeting the population's basic material needs eventually leads to societal groups demanding political participation to further their interests. The reduced insulation accompanying democratisation and the need to take greater account of cross cutting internal societal concerns and external pressure has therefore affected the extent to which top policy makers are able to quickly and effectively change policy if they wish to maintain support. While the maintenance of legitimacy has always required attention to broader societal concerns, the greater pressure that democratic institutions and processes places upon policy makers can make the difference between effective and ineffective policy reform.

This work adds to this analysis by emphasising the point that bureaucratic capacity is affected by changes in the state's political capacity. As interest groups increase their ability to permeate the policy making processes of the state, they are able to exacerbate any division which already exists over policy direction or create divisions concerning the appropriate course of future policy. It is here that leadership, institutions and ideology as determinants of policy change again become important. As interest groups increase their ability to participate, it becomes more difficult to develop a dominant ideology and more difficult for leadership to act except in relation to particular issues where society is carried along with the state's goals. At the same time there may be a need to reform institutions to enable them to react to the changed relations between the state and society but this too becomes more difficult in a democratic setting. The result is that reform on various issues at various times may only be possible when windows of opportunity occur.

This book commences in Chapter one with a discussion of the major competing approaches which top policy makers can adopt to foreign investment policy. The first of these can be described as an interventionist approach. In this approach, policy instruments are necessary to steer foreign investment into sectors targeted for development and to ensure that foreign firms act as learning agents for local firms. The second approach is a market oriented one. This approach relies on the market mechanism as the primary determinant of the supply and sectoral allocation of foreign investment in the economy in the host state. It has already been noted that commencing in 1980 policy makers attempted to change from a highly interventionist approach to a more market oriented approach. The debate concerning the appropriate policy orientation towards foreign investment has been at the core of policy difficulties since that time. It has been a central reason for the conflicting views within the bureaucracy and between internal societal groups and external actors on this issue and has therefore played a significant role in the reduction of state capacity in relation to it. This chapter therefore lays the foundation for the discussion which follows concerning the Korean state's capacity for policy change.

Chapter two sets out the policy measures taken by the state in the 1960s and 1970s. It demonstrates that the interventionist policy stance was effective in terms of delivering outcomes which accorded with policy makers' objectives. Foreign investment policy consisted of a range of specific policy instruments which effectively confined foreign investment to areas which were seen by policy makers as development priorities at the time. Policies were effective because they ensured that foreign investment contributed to the development of key Korean industries and because Korea avoided some of the negative side effects that can occur from unfettered flows of foreign investment. The effectiveness of policy outcomes provides a significant part of the explanation for the reluctance of bureaucrats to abandon their interventionist stance when, in 1980, key policy makers attempted to move towards a free market approach.

Chapter three examines the underlying basis for the Korean state's capacity to effectively manage foreign investment in the 1960s and 1970s. The Korean developmental state of the Park Chung Hee era exhibited a high level of bureaucratic capacity and political capacity in relation to economic policy of which foreign investment policy was a part. Bureaucratic capacity arose out of the leadership that Park and his political appointees demonstrated on economic policy issues and the institutional configuration of the state where a key economic agency, the Economic Planning Board, maintained coordination of policy amongst economic ministries and resolved conflicts concerning it. The political capacity of Park's developmental state rested upon a development coalition with big business groups in which the state was the dominant partner and the exclusion of other societal actors from direct involvement in policy processes. At the same time, the state's policy makers faced few constraints from the external environment on this issue. The state's bureaucratic capacity and political capacity were significantly enhanced by the dissemination and wide acceptance of an ideology of developmentalism. Park was able to channel nationalistic sentiments into a national drive for economic growth which not only assisted in maintaining cohesiveness within the state but also provided his regime with a measure of legitimacy.

Chapter four explains the reduced capacity of the state to achieve desired policy outcomes in relation to foreign investment during the time of the Chun administration. In the early 1980s, the capacity of the state for effective policy change diminished with the consequence that the objectives of key policy makers were not realised. The diminution in state capacity arose initially from a division within the state concerning the future direction of economic policy. Top policy makers advocated a more open market approach while ordinary bureaucrats were unwilling to abandon the interventionist policies of the past. New institutional arrangements concerning foreign investment and constraints which the leadership faced in resolving the difference of opinion emerging within the bureaucratic institutions of the state undermined the cohesiveness of the bureaucracy on this issue. The continuation of the Park regime's practice of excluding most societal actors from policy processes led to the state maintaining relative insulation from societal pressures during this time. The internal institutions of the executive branch of the state dominated policy processes with business groups in a subservient yet consultative role.

Chapter five argues that the ideological split on this issue was unable to be resolved by the Roh regime because of legitimacy, leadership and structural constraints. Despite a commonality of interests between big business, foreign actors and top policy makers for general deregulatory measures early in the regime, little policy change occurred. This highlights the significant structural power of the bureaucracy at the working level of policy formulation and implementation to block change in a direction which they opposed. The position of the bureaucrats was reinforced by the increased ability of societal groups to express their opposition to a more market oriented policy position. In the newly democratised environment the national assembly, as the elected representatives of the population, and the labour movement were prepared to be more vocal in pursuing the demands of their constituents. The democratised environment required the state to respond to internal demands in the interests of maintaining support. The conflicting internal and external demands led to difficulties in policy reform. The institutional arrangements that were adopted during the Roh era reduced the prospects of reconciling competing demands leaving lower level bureaucrats to continue to pursue their own interests in seeking to maintain an interventionist approach.

The final chapter argues that the changes that have been able to occur in foreign investment policy in recent years have been as a result of a restoration of state capacity in relation to this issue. Strong leadership together with a lack of opposition from business groups to deregulation have been partially responsible for the significant changes which have occurred in the foreign investment policy area. These factors have been reinforced by institutional changes that the Kim administration has made in relation to foreign investment and the greater control which the administration has been able to exercise over the national assembly. At the same time the state has been able to overcome societal opposition with a concerted attempt to implant a new ideology of internationalisation in the minds of the bureaucracy and the population at large to replace the old ideology of developmentalism and the highly interventionist role for the state that it implied. While the state has exhibited renewed capacity in relation to issues concerned with internationalisation and achieved some deregulation in relation to them, the long held view within the bureaucracy that the state should play a leading role in directing economic activity has meant that the government's aim for more general deregulation has not been achieved to the same extent.

It is necessary at this point to clarify several of the key terms used throughout this work. The term Korea is used for convenience to refer to the Republic of Korea or South Korea. Foreign investment refers to foreign direct investment. Foreign investment has been consistently defined in the Foreign Capital Inducement Laws as including any level of ownership by foreigners in a Korean company ranging from wholly foreign owned through to majority owned or minority shares. In practical terms most foreign investors require a level of ownership that guarantees them a degree of control over the firm's operations. Accordingly minority ownership by foreigners usually occurs in a joint venture arrangement between a Korean firm and a foreign firm in which the foreigner may hold less than half the shares but still exercise some management rights. The term foreign investment is used throughout this book with both the formal definition and its practical limitations in mind.

The term policy makers is also used extensively. The level of the bureaucracy which is closest to the initiation and implementation of foreign investment policy is the Foreign Investment Division currently located in the Ministry of Finance and Economy. Prior to that, it was located in the Ministry of Finance and before 1981 in the Economic Planning Board. Other ministries, particularly the Ministry of Trade and Industry, have always been consulted in both the formulation and implementation phases. In addition the opinions of specialist research institutes are often taken into account.

Changes in policy are drafted in the Foreign Investment Division proceed to the head of the division and then to the vice minister and on to the minister. At this level of top policy making ministers may work with the president's economic advisers. The president may become involved depending on the importance of the issue. Those policy matters which involve amendments of laws must be passed by the national assembly before the president gives final assent. While there are therefore many parts of the bureaucracy and political leadership which are involved in the formulation and implementation of foreign investment policy, key policy makers are those senior bureaucrats, government ministers and personnel in the presidential office, including the president, who become involved.

Finally a note on methodology. This study proceeded by way of identification of the theoretical literature on institutionalist theory and on foreign investment in Korea. This was supplemented by the use of newspaper and magazine articles which provided assessments of developments in policy and reasons for them at the time that they occurred. Field work was undertaken in Korea at various times in 1994, 1995 and 1996. Interviews were conducted with government officials, representatives of peak industry associations private agencies and law firms which have extensive dealings with foreign investors as well as a number of prominent academics and representatives of major research institutes. Use has also been made of literature in the Korean language on foreign investment policy.

1 'State' and 'Market' Approaches to Foreign Investment Policy

Introduction

The approach that policy makers adopt towards foreign investment tends toward either an interventionist or a more market oriented stance. These alternative policy orientations have their basis in statist theory and neoclassical theory. The approach that a particular set of policy makers adopts may well depend upon the extent to which they accept the underlying assumptions and principles involved in either approach.

Economic policy is not made in a vacuum. Those who are charged with the task of policy making have views and assumptions of their own as to which pathway should be chosen to economic development. These views are conditioned not only by cultural values but also by educational experiences, the domestic and international economic and political environment and perceptions of the success or failure of previous policy initiatives. The transmission of policy relevant knowledge occurs across international boundaries and results in policy makers also learning from the policy successes and failures of other states.

This chapter sets out the underlying assumptions and principles for each policy approach. As noted by Rasiah (1995) the neoclassical approach has perhaps been the dominant paradigm in the literature on foreign investment policy. For this reason this chapter seeks to develop the statist approach in a little more detail.

The purpose of this chapter is to lay the foundations for later chapters which show that Korean policy makers in the 1960s and 1970s adopted an interventionist approach to foreign investment but in the early 1980s sought to abandon this in favour of a more market oriented policy. Differences in view developed as to which strategy was the more appropriate. Much of the debate which has occurred concerning policy since that time has centred around the differences inherent in each approach and the effect that each has on the interests of various participants in policy processes.

9

A Market Oriented Approach to Foreign Direct Investment

A market oriented approach to foreign investment policy is based on assumptions made by neoclassical theorists concerning the role of the state in economic development. Using the works of Smith and Ricardo as their basis, proponents of this school of thought believe that the optimal path to economic development occurs when the state plays a minimalist role, confining itself to the provision of a stable economic and political environment in which free enterprise guided by the market produces the goods and services which lead to improvement of the community's welfare (Reidel 1988: 35–7). The state is seen as limiting its function to the provision of public goods, a stable and predictable macro economic environment and a free trade regime. State intervention should only occur to correct clear cases of market failure (Islam 1994: 93; Wade 1991: 11) relying on the market mechanism as the ultimate arbiter of production.

A fundamental requirement for the proper functioning of the market mechanism is the existence of competition between firms. Neoclassical theorists recognise that in certain limited circumstances markets may fail in adequately providing competition. In those circumstances, there may be a case for government intervention in the form of competition laws to ensure that goods and services are available at the lowest possible price in the interests of maximising the overall welfare of the community.

Neoclassical theory is extended to the international arena by the assumption that different states have different factor endowments and for this reason some states will be more efficient at producing some goods rather than others. States are therefore said to have a comparative advantage in the production of those goods which their factor endowments allow to be produced more cheaply than in other states. International trade is the mechanism by which states exchange those goods in which they have a comparative advantage for those goods in which they have a comparative disadvantage. It is therefore in the best interests of community welfare for states not to interfere in the free flow of goods and services across state boundaries.

In pure neoclassical theory then, there should be no reason for firms to establish operations in other countries (Krugman 1983: 57). In a world where each country efficiently produces goods and services in accordance with its comparative advantage, those goods and services should be able to be traded without firms having to move across country boundaries. In order to explain the phenomenon of foreign direct investment, neoclassical theory has to resort to explanations which, in theoretical terms are second best.

These have proceeded down a number of different pathways but in recent times Dunning's eclectic theory of international production has perhaps provided the most comprehensive framework for the analysis of the determinants of foreign investment (UNCTC 1992a). Drawing together various theoretical approaches which had been developed by earlier writers, Dunning (1988) hypothesised that there are three sets of factors which determine international production. The first of these he called ownership advantages. In the course of their operations some firms acquire particular advantages such as marketing skills, research and development skills or production skills which allow them to become more competitive than their rivals within the same industry. The acquisition of these advantages means they are able to provide goods and services more competitively not only in their own country but also in other countries. In order to exploit these advantages firms invest overseas despite the obstacles faced by the firm in operating in a different cultural and regulatory environment.

The second element of Dunning's theory explains why firms invest to exploit their ownership advantages rather than simply exporting the product or entering into licensing arrangements or strategic alliances. The explanation relates to the transaction costs which arise in international trade transactions. These can be simple transport costs, different rates of taxes and charges from country to country or other market imperfections which make it more profitable for a firm to exploit its ownership advantages by locating in the overseas country rather than selling direct or licensing the technology to firms in the host country. The third element of Dunning's theory seeks to explain why firms choose to invest in one country rather than another. He argues that certain features of a host country's natural and policy environment lead firms to choose that country in preference to others. Location advantages, as Dunning calls them, include natural resources, domestic market potential, labour costs, political stability and government policies which affect the economic environment in which the firm operates.

Although foreign investment is a second best option in theoretical terms, it can still confer a benefit on the host country through its operation as a resource transfer (Hill and Johns 1991; Ahiakpor 1991; Helleiner 1991). A resource transfer approach places emphasis on aggregate flows of foreign investment to a recipient country. The positive benefits to the recipient country not only include an addition of capital, but also flow from the foreign firms' ownership advantages of advanced technology, increased ability to penetrate overseas markets, employment growth and backward and forward linkages (Johnson H.G. 1967: 61; Thirlwall 1972: 263; Islam and Chowdhury 1993; Hill and Johns 1991; Parry 1988; Ahaiakpor 1991). It is assumed that any negative side effects of foreign investment such as the crowding out of local investors will be counteracted by the fact that foreign investment will only flow into those areas where it has a comparative advantage. This leads to the country as a whole being better off with local industries specialising in areas where they have a comparative advantage offsetting any specific disadvantages of particular firms.

The neoclassical position is that policies which attempt to steer foreign investment into selected sectors of the economy will lead to distortions in the allocation of scarce foreign capital resources and will lead to a risk of 'government failure' in their allocation. It is argued that the government does not know where foreign investment can be most productive in the economy (Goldsmith 1995: 647). This decision is best determined by firms themselves. Consequently the government should confine itself to providing a conducive policy environment such as realistic exchange rates, free movement of foreign capital, competitive interest and tax rates and minimal bureaucratic interference in the foreign investment process (Rasiah 1995: 11; Lee H.K. 1994).

Negative effects of foreign investment are due to inappropriate government macro economic and industry policies of which foreign investment policies are a small subset (Parry 1988: 122; Johnson H.G. 1967: 61–2). Results of these policies may be either monopolies or highly protected and inefficient local or foreign invested firms. Host countries can avoid these negative effects by way of suitable general policies. Refraining from protecting any sector whether through foreign investment policies or more general industry policies will prevent inefficiencies from arising (Fry 1993(b): 61–2).

Foreign investment policy in the form of either incentive or restrictive measures is criticised by neoclassical theorists. Restrictive foreign investment policy measures which, for example, seek to confine it to certain industries or set limits on levels of foreign ownership in any project are criticised on a number of grounds. At the outset it is argued that they deter foreign investors thereby reducing investment flows and depriving the country of the advantages which it brings. It was the acceptance of this point of view by policy makers in many developing countries including Korea which led to attempts by key policy makers to reduce restrictive measures at the beginning of the 1980s (Contractor 1990; Aranda 1988).

Restrictive measures are also criticised because they amount to no more than devices to protect domestic industry from foreign competition. As such they are argued to be subject to the same failings as all protectionist devices which lead to rent seeking by narrowly based interest groups leading to a lower level of overall community welfare than that which would have been possible in their absence (Matthews and Ravenhill

1994: 71). In extreme cases policies which seek to distort foreign investment flows in this way may lead to decreases in overall welfare (Naya and Ramstetter 1988: 66; Fry 1993(b): 19).

Those who seek to reduce protection do so because of acceptance of the argument that protection benefits narrow sections of society at the expense of society generally. Protection has the tendency to lead to inefficient firms which are not internationally competitive thereby depriving society at large of goods and services at least cost. While key policy makers may recognise this argument, it is more difficult to implement because of the interests which arise from protectionist policies. It is here that the capacity of the state is crucial. This will become apparent in later chapters which deal with the attempts by top policy makers to reduce protectionist measures in Korea in the 1980s.

While criticism of restrictive foreign investment policies has proceeded under the banner of general criticisms of protectionist policies, there is more specific research to support the neoclassical position that foreign investment policy in the form of investment incentives should be avoided. Rather, various features of the investment environment provide a far stronger explanation. Lim (1994: 837) summarises the position as follows:

> Empirical studies show that there is no support for the belief of the governments of most developing countries that the provision of fiscal incentives is necessary to attract direct foreign investment. Nor is there support for the belief that the greater the generosity of the incentive programs, the greater will be the level of investment. What matters are the presence of natural resources and the pursuit of sound economic policies. The latter would include the type of fiscal monetary and budgetary policies that lead to high savings.

A large number of studies undertaken over the past two decades have tended to show that incentives are not a major determinant of foreign investment flows. One of earlier studies was that of Root and Ahmed (1978) who carried out a study of 41 developing countries categorising them as unattractive, moderately attractive and highly attractive based on the amount of investment that had entered these countries between 1966 and 1970. They found that there were six variables which explained the differences in investment flows. Tax incentives were not one of them. Agodo (1979) studied the investment decisions of 33 firms in African countries and concluded that tax concessions were insignificant in influencing their decisions to invest.

In 1983, Lim published a study in which he investigated patterns of investment for 27 developing countries. He used regression analysis to test the significance of natural resources, level of economic development, rate of economic growth and tax incentives as influences on foreign investment flows. He found that all variables other than tax incentives were positively related to foreign investment flows. He also concluded that the level of generosity of tax incentives was negatively related to the amount of foreign investment and explained this by saying that fiscal hyper generosity in the form of tax incentives was seen as a danger signal and not as a lure (Lim 1983: 210).

In 1984 the Group of Thirty conducted a study concerning the effect of tax incentives on the decision by 52 international corporations to invest in 12 different countries. In his report of this study, Helleiner (1991: 148) notes that not one corporation was found to have listed tax incentives in their top three reasons for investing. However, there was some recognition that in cases where all other factors were approximately equal, tax incentives, while not a major reason for investing, might tip the balance in favour of a particular country.

Sheperd, Silbertson and Strange (1985) found in their survey of investment by British companies that tax regulations and government incentives had negligible effects. Dunning (1986) also found in his survey of Japanese firms investing in the UK that incentives and foreign investment policy only had a modest influence. O'Sullivan's (1985) study of foreign investment in Ireland during 1960–79 found that the primary determinants were labour costs, the exchange rate and market size. Fiscal incentives were not statistically significant.

A study by the United Nations Centre for Transnational Corporations to determine which variables had the greatest influence on foreign investment flows selected 46 countries (21 developed countries; 5 newly industrialising countries and 20 less developed countries); 7 investment policy variables (tax incentives, ownership policies, convertibility of foreign exchange, price controls, performance requirements, application and other procedures and sector specific controls) and 3 macro economic variables (market size, political risk ratings and the exchange rate) (UNCTC 1991). It was hypothesised that announced policy changes in the seven policy categories might positively affect foreign investment flows or that investment flow might be positively associated with the market size or the growth rate of the economy. Correlation and regression analysis showed that, for the most part, changes in foreign investment policy including incentives had only a weak and scattered influence on investment flows. However, restrictive measures in the form of performance requirements, were found to negatively affect foreign investment flows for industrialised and newly industrialising countries. It was also found that a 'more powerful explanation of investment flows was the size and growth rate of the host country economy' (UNCTC, 1991: 59).

Pfefferman (1991: 218–19) summarised a study by the International Finance Corporation on the effect of tax incentives for both export oriented investment and domestic market oriented investment. It found that in 38 export oriented investments, incentives ranked in the top three reasons in 15 cases. In 36 domestic market oriented investments incentives ranked in the top 3 reasons in only 2 cases. This led to the conclusion that incentives have little influence in domestic market oriented investments but may have a bearing on the investment decision in export oriented projects.

The findings of these studies supports the proposition that investment incentives are not an important determinant of investment flows. In their study of the impact of incentives on investment decisions by both domestic and foreign firms, Boadway and Shah (1992: 26) point out that the major limitation of tax incentives for foreign investors is that while tax exemptions for foreign firms may lead to less tax in the host country, they will more often than not lead to the firm paying the tax in its home country. For that reason firms do not consider incentives to be important.

The specific evidence for Korea is confined to survey type studies which are subject to criticism as mentioned below. However the studies that have been undertaken generally support the findings set out above.

Lee (1980) refers to two surveys which were carried out in the 1970s. The first of these by Chu in 1975, surveyed both US and Japanese firms concerning their motives for investing in Korea. Tax incentives were not mentioned as a significant factor. The most important factor was the cost of labour, followed by the growth rate of the economy and the size of the domestic market. The second survey was carried out by Chung in 1976. It is the only survey for Korea which rates tax incentives as an important factor in investment decisions by foreign firms. Chung found that cheap labour was of secondary importance to the incentives offered by the Korean government.

Further surveys were carried out in the 1980s. Koo and Bark (1988) refer to a survey carried out by the Korea Industrial Research Institute in 1985. The survey results showed that the overwhelming motivation for investors was that of accessing the domestic market. Eighty five (85 per cent) of the firms surveyed identified this as their primary motive. Other significant reasons included the use of Korea as an export platform (61.8 per cent); cheap labour (38.2 per cent); good technological capability (20.6 per cent) and others, including tax incentives, (17.6 per cent). It is clear that factors associated with the investment environment rated much more significantly than tax incentives.

These results are consistent with a survey conducted by Cho (1984). He surveyed US companies investing in Korea and reports that 77 per cent did so to expand their market for goods. Only 7 per cent invested because of the lower costs. Thus incentives, as a part of the factors which lower costs, did not rate highly. In 1991 a further survey was carried out by the Ministry of Finance (MOF 1993). It was found that 43 per cent of the firms surveyed indicated that the domestic market was the major motivation for investment. Only 4 per cent of those surveyed mentioned tax privileges as a reason for investing (MOF 1993: 566).

It is difficult to find more general studies to show conclusively that incentives do positively affect foreign investment flows. A survey of manufacturing firms by Reuber in 1973 showed that 48 per cent of respondents would have abandoned their investment plans in export oriented areas had it not been for the incentives offered (Reuber 1973). However, survey studies of this type are criticised by neoclassical theorists because they fail to survey firms which do not invest and therefore do not establish the true impact of incentives on the investment decision (Boadway and Shah 1992: 73).

A study by Guisinger (1985) of 74 cases of investment by manufacturing companies in Latin America in the automobile, food, computer and petrochemical industries found that in 'two thirds of the cases surveyed, the choice of country was influenced by host country policy' (Guisinger 1985: 317). However, as noted by Pfefferman (1991: 218–19), Guisinger's study adopted such a broad range of possible incentive measures it was not possible to isolate the relative influence of tax and other direct financial inducements from more general features of the host country's policy environment.

The studies set out above have formed the basis of opinions of development related bodies such as the International Monetary Fund (IMF), the Organisation for Economic Cooperation and Development (OECD) and the World Bank which advise against the use of investment incentives (IMF 1985; OECD 1983, 1993; World Bank 1987, 1993, 1994). However while they consistently argue that incentives stand well below other features of the investment environment in the foreign investment decision, there is some recognition by all of them that incentives may be of influence if it comes down to a choice of location between competing countries with similar investment environments.

For example, the OECD (1983: 45) suggested that incentives might affect regional allocation patterns of investment. The UNCTC agrees that 'once a company has reached a point of deciding to invest in one of a small number of very similar countries then incentives might tip the balance towards a particular location' (UNCTC 1992(a): 60). This point is also supported by other observers. Gold (1991: 23) suggests that incentives might tip the balance in favour of one country rather than another if all other considerations are roughly equal. Weigand (1986: 147) also argues that the need to stay ahead of competitors is a reason for host countries to offer incentives to potential foreign investors.

This issue is of importance because there has continued to be a view that Korea must continue to offer incentives to keep up with competitors. As will be seen, this view has been an integral part of the approach to foreign investment adopted by those parts of the bureaucracy in Korea which favour a more interventionist stance. Those who favour a neoclassical view however, tend to argue that the occasions on which incentives might make a difference are rare indeed and therefore do not justify their use (Helleiner 1991: 148; Kim W.S. and Lee K.C.: 176–80).

An Interventionist Approach to Foreign Direct Investment

The alternative framework which policy makers can adopt to foreign investment follows from a view that the state has a significant role to play in the development process. Thus, in relation to foreign investment, the state has a role to play in channelling it into those industries which are considered as significant for overall development at various times. It has been noted that during the 1960s and 1970s Korean policy makers adopted this approach.

It is therefore necessary to set out in some detail the assumptions that such an approach implies as these differ markedly from the assumptions that are implied in a neoclassical approach. For this reason there is likely to be considerable difficulties for policy makers should they wish to change from an interventionist policy style to a more market oriented approach. These difficulties arise not only because vested interests benefiting from interventionist measures will have been built up in sections of society and in the bureaucracy but also because it is difficult for political leaders to change the mindset of the bureaucracy from one of playing a managing role to a laissez faire approach in which there is limited room for the state.

Those who favoured a highly interventionist role for the state in the economic development of Korea and Taiwan based their approach on the experience of other late industrialising countries such as Germany and Japan. In those countries development occurred through a process of learning from the more advanced countries of the era in order to catch up in the industrialisation process (Gerschenkron 1955; Hirschman 1958; White and Wade 1984; Amsden 1989; Wade 1991; Johnson 1987, 1992,

1994; Matthews and Ravenhill 1994: 65). The process of learning had involved a central role for the state in development planning and in the allocation and mobilisation of the resources necessary to realise the plans. Late industrialisers differed from centrally planned economies in that they allowed the market to work in the determination of supply and demand but did not rely on the market mechanism to allocate resources (Amsden 1989: 11).

A statist approach therefore challenges the assumption that competitive forces rather than government intervention will result in the unleashing of free enterprise activity leading to economic growth and development (Chang 1993: 145; Chang and Wright 1994: 859–64). Rather, a review of the experiences of late industrialisers tended to show that competition had been restricted in the interests of ensuring that the scarce resources available for development were not employed in ways which adversely affected the realisation of the goals set out in economic plans (Chang 1993: 140). Further, the experience of late developers showed a willingness to protect infant industries from the forces of foreign competition until those industries reached a stage where they were internationally competitive. At the same time those firms which did not meet performance standards set by the state no longer received the support of the state (Chang 1993: 148). The state's ability to carry through this method of discipline depended very much on the capacity of the state for effective intervention.

The assumption concerning comparative advantage that is made by those favouring a free market approach is also challenged by those believing in a more interventionist role for the state. The neoclassical view is that economic development occurs through allowing initial factor endowments to determine comparative advantage and changes to it occurring through increased international trade. Statists tend to the view that a county's dynamic comparative advantage is determined by the extent to which it is able to absorb, adapt and improve on the technology, production and marketing methods of more advanced countries (Wade 1992: 297–8). There is therefore a role for the state in building the necessary absorptive capacity for this to occur.

These assumptions concerning the development process imply a significant role for the state in planning, allocating resources to priority industries pursuant to such plans and building the absorptive capacity of society to enhance its learning capability. The history of late developers shows that states vary in their capacity to undertake these tasks. It is for this reason that the issue of state capacity is of fundamental importance in determining development outcomes and the harnessing of foreign resources to assist in the development process.

The Capacity of the State to Manage Foreign Investment

The capacity of the state to utilise foreign resources as a part of the overall development process depends upon its bureaucratic capacity for policy formulation and implementation, its autonomy from societal actors and the degree to which it is constrained by external forces and events (Evans 1985; Evans and Rueschemeyer, 1985; Skocpol 1985; Evans 1992; Kim E.M. 1993; Haggard 1988; 1994; Haggard and Moon 1992). It is worth reiterating here that bureaucratic capacity refers to the ability of the bureaucracy to competently and cohesively formulate and implement policy leading to outcomes which accord with the objectives of policy makers. Political capacity or autonomy as it has sometimes been called refers to the ability of the state to formulate policies independently of the direct influence of interest groups.

The examination of the capacity of the state to effectively intervene to harness foreign investment to the development goals of the state has not been undertaken in much depth in the literature. Krasner (1978) and Katzenstein (1978) noted the significance of state capacity in determining outcomes in their analysis of more general foreign policy issues in industrialised countries. The issue was also addressed in some studies of the role of the state in relation to foreign capital in Latin American countries (Evans 1979; Stepan 1978). However, while Haggard (1988), Evans (1987) Stallings (1991) Kim E.M. (1992) and Woo J.E. (1991) have all examined the role of foreign capital in East Asia none have dealt in any depth with the issue of the variability of state capacity in relation to foreign investment.

A major contribution has been made by Clark and Chan (1994, 1995(a) and 1995(b)) to the understanding of the interventionist role played by many states in the East Asian region towards foreign investment. They have put forward a number of arguments concerning the capacity of East Asian states in dealing with multinational corporations. They argue at the outset that it is the capacity of the state which determines the extent to which multinational corporations (MNC) participate in economic activity within host states. States which have a relatively high level of state capacity, or strong states, as they refer to them, have the potential to either limit MNC participation or allow it to represent a considerable force in any sector. In this regard Clark and Chan contrast strong states, such as Korea which has strictly limited MNC access in the past, with states such as Singapore which have allowed a significant presence of multinational corporations. On the other hand, weak states such as the Philippines which are either not insulated in policy making on this issue or demonstrate low levels of bureaucratic capacity in relation to foreign capital have not had effective control over MNC access (Clark and Chan 1995 (a): 93–7).

They argue that state capacity also determines whether MNC's will have a positive or negative impact on the host country's economy. In this they have support from Lall and Streeten's study of over 30 countries which found that state capacity had a considerable bearing on the type of impact that multinational corporations would have on host states economies (Lall and Streeten 1977: 222). The issue of impact is separate from the issue of access, in that states with high levels of capacity have been able to derive benefits from multinational participation even though the level of access is low in some cases, such as Korea, and high in others such as Singapore. However countries which have low levels of capacity to deal with multinational corporations, such as the Philippines, tend to exhibit adverse impacts (Clark and Chan 1995 (a): 97; 1994: 344).

A further element of their argument is to analyse the determinants of state capacity in relation to multinational corporations (Chan and Clark 1995: 177–18). They define the state's capacity in this regard as 'coping capacity'. They make the following observation:

> These considerations lead us to argue that coping capacity, that is the ability to exploit and indeed create opportunities, is more the result of the collaborative synergies between the state and society and of the governments ability to take advantage of the MNC's assets for national development (Chan and Clark 1995: 180).

Clark and Chan therefore implicitly recognise political capacity and bureaucratic capacity as the elements of a state's coping capacity in relation to foreign investment. They also make some observations concerning the determinants of coping capacity. They argue that coping capacity depends upon the political-economy culture of the country concerned in that cultural norms and values influence not only official policies but also the way in which local firms, and the workforce generally, respond to the presence of multinational corporations (Clark and Chan 1995b: 99). It is therefore cultural norms which underpin the ability of the state to harness multinational corporations for development purposes.

While Clark and Chan's arguments are largely accepted here, it is suggested that a state's capacity in relation to foreign investment does not so much depend primarily upon political culture but upon the ability of policy makers to utilise the existing political-cultural predispositions of its own society to enhance its autonomy and bureaucratic capacity. While cultural norms underlie the structure of state society relations (Risse Kappen 1995: 21), it is the manner in which they reinforce the state's ability to insulate itself from internal societal pressures and enhance its bureaucratic capacity that are determinative of patterns of MNC access and impact.

Thus a country's 'coping capacity' as defined by Clark and Chan needs further analysis according to each specific country. In any such analysis it is useful to explore the determinants of both bureaucratic capacity and political capacity. Bureaucratic capacity determines the state's bargaining power with multinational corporations and therefore the outcomes from foreign investment. Provided that the state has the necessary bureaucratic capacity it is able to effectively utilise a combination of incentive and restrictive measures in bargaining with foreign investors (Stoever 1989: 68; IMF 1985; Gold 1991: 23; Behrman and Grosse 1990: 103; Guisinger 1985; OECD 1983, 1989; Weigel 1988: 5–9) in order to obtain a trade off between what the state wants to gain and what foreign investors will tolerate (Lall and Streeten 1977; 209–12; Vernon 1971).

Restrictive measures include the limiting of foreign investment to selected industries to either protect local infant industry or to seek to steer foreign investment into certain areas of the economy which are seen as priorities for development. Restrictive measures often play a role in the actual bargaining process with foreign investors in that the host state may either prescribe, or leave open to negotiations, levels of foreign equity, local content requirements, export minimums, the extent to which capital may be borrowed locally or externally and conditions to ensure that technology, management and marketing skills are transferred to local firms. Incentive measures also play a role in the bargaining process. They frequently include tax or import duty concessions for foreign firms, the provision of special industrial facilities and privileged access to capital markets. Because of perceived competition for foreign investment and in an attempt to offset some of the restrictions that they need to impose for developmental reasons, many host states, including Korea, have maintained an elaborate package of financial incentives (Encarnation and Wells 1985: 48).

The ability to obtain effective outcomes from foreign investment also depends on the extent to which the state is insulated from societal actors (Krasner 1995: 276). The effective formulation and implementation of foreign investment policy requires input from business groups and therefore a certain degree of embeddedness of the state within society while at the same time insulation from their particularistic demands. As Doner (1992: 145) notes, in order for the state to play an effective role in screening foreign investment proposals, it needs expert advice from the business sector while at the same time being in a position to resist business pressure for particularistic advantages from foreign investment projects.

On the other hand it also requires the containment of societal opposition. Few issues arouse the public sentiment more than foreign multinational corporations controlling scarce resources and appropriating the benefits of their exploitation for themselves. Legitimacy concerns often demand that policy makers be able to demonstrate that foreign capital is playing a positive role. Opposition to foreign investment may only be able to be contained if positive outcomes occur from the participation by foreign capital and if society at large is carried along with the state's overriding developmental ideology.

The state's capacity to mange foreign investment over time may therefore depend on such positive outcomes occurring. The specific contributions that foreign investment can make and their limitations therefore need some analysis in order to more fully appreciate the difficulties inherent in an interventionist approach.

Encouraging Learning through Transfer of Technology and
International Marketing Skills

One of the major benefits that policy makers in developing countries hope to achieve from foreign investment is the upgrading of the technological capability of local firms. Because of the sequencing strategy that late industrialisers often adopt to economic development (Shin 1991: 52; Yeom 1994: Amsden 1989), the industries where foreign firms can most usefully contribute will vary over time. Thus the state allocates foreign investment to those industries seen as priorities in the particular stage of industrialisation that the country has reached at the time.

The development of technological capability in an industry involves acquisition of the technology from foreign firms, diffusion of it throughout the industry concerned and finally its improvement by local firms (Kim Linsu 1980: 256–7). Foreign investment can therefore play a major role in the acquisition and diffusion stages of local firms' development of technological capability. Over time, the types of technology that firms in a particular industry wish to acquire varies in line with the development of the industry. Firms first import what Kim and Dahlman (1992) have called mature technology products. This means that local firms learn to make the products that foreign firms have developed in their home countries. Following the mature phase is the consolidation phase, where local firms import technology for the purpose of improving their methods of production to make them more cost effective thereby increasing their competitive advantage. Finally, technology is imported to assist in the development of state of the art products. In each stage, local firms seek to acquire the technology by means of foreign investment or other sources.

There are a number of alternatives for local firms for the acquisition of foreign technology. The simplest method occurs through the usage, maintenance and reverse engineering of imported capital goods and their adaptation for local conditions. There is also the possibility of relying upon overseas journals or visits overseas by technical staff for either informal or formal training so that they become acquainted with foreign technology and can then come home and duplicate it (Enos 1989: 7). Such processes often infringe the intellectual property rights of the original producer and for this reason governments of developing countries often face pressure to resort to more formal and legal means to acquire technology. This has occurred in recent years in Korea as Byun and Wang (1994: 3) note.

Formal means include the acquisition of technology through turnkey projects where overseas companies construct an industrial facility to operation stage and then train local operators before handing the plant over to them. Alternatively technology can be acquired through licence arrangements or strategic alliances thereby avoiding a permanent foreign presence in the industry (Hong 1994: 2–3). However when it comes to the acquisition of state of the art technology, these informal and formal means will often be inadequate. Foreign firms will guard their innovations closely and may not be prepared to either licence the technology for fear of competition or enter into strategic alliances. Foreign investment may therefore be the only alternative for countries seeking to develop high technology industries on a par with those in advanced industrialised countries. This point has consistently been recognised by policy makers in Korea. However, differences have arisen about how the technology benefits from foreign investment can best be captured.

There are many potential benefits to local firms which flow from exposure to more advanced technologies. The first of these is the introduction of local firms to more efficient and cost effective methods of operation thereby increasing their profitability (Byun and Wang 1994: 2). This may occur through local firms entering into joint ventures with foreign firms or alternatively through acting as suppliers to multinational firms and thereby acquiring access to more efficient or cost effective ways of manufacturing or providing services. A second possible method of learning occurs through workers at technical levels moving out of the employ of multinationals into the employ of local firms and bringing with them the more advanced methods that they have learnt in the foreign firm. A third possible method is through the indirect effect of competition. If multinational firms move into an industry with their more advanced management and production methods, local firms may be prompted to upgrade their own technology levels in order to compete (Moran 1978: 86–7).

While it is acknowledged that there are many potential benefits to local firms from exposure to more advanced technologies (Hill and Johns 1991; Byun and Wang 1994: 1; Singer and Ansari 1977: 195; Cohen 1975: 22; Lall and Streeten 1977: 178), there is no guarantee that local firms will automatically acquire the ability to innovate rather than simply imitate or adapt the production processes utilised by more advanced countries (Lall and Streeten 1977: 66–7; Reuber 1973). There is a school of thought which suggests that foreign investment may even work against the ability of a country to reach the innovative stage of product development in lines of products where foreign firms dominate domestic industry.

This occurs because of the tendency of foreign firms to be unwilling to carry out the research and development necessary for product innovation in the local economy both because they do not wish to run the risk of their ownership advantages being appropriated by local firms and because it is more efficient to confine such operations to their centralised headquarters (Lall and Streeten 1977: 56–7; Singer and Ansari 1975: 204–5; Evans 1979: 35: Hymer and Rowthorn 1979: 50). In these circumstances local firms receive the results of innovations rather than learning to innovate themselves (Lall 1992). Evans (1979: 290–8) gives examples of the tendency of foreign firms to transfer already well developed technologies in basic industries such as steel, textiles and chemicals thereby not contributing much to local firms' ability to innovate.

Following this is a pattern of foreign firms establishing operations in developing countries to produce products which it is no longer cost effective to produce in the home country (Vernon 1966; Singer and Ansari 1975: 195; Hymer and Rowthorn 1976: 47; Newfarmer 1983: 178). The technology embodied in such products is often not at the leading edge in the industry concerned and consequently the potential for host country firms to move up the technology ladder is diminished. Where foreign firms dominate a number of key industries this may lead to the development of a branch plant mentality in the host country whereby local firms are only ever producing goods for overseas markets sometimes with outdated machinery which has been physically transferred from the home country to the host country (Hymer 1976: 49; Lall and Streeten 1977: 58).

There is also the possibility that even if technology that is introduced is of a kind which might benefit local firms, they may be precluded from taking advantage of it because foreign firms insist on the strict enforcement of intellectual property laws in the host country to maintain their ownership advantages which led them to invest in the first place. Alternatively local firms might lack the relevant knowledge to be able to utilise this technology even if there is leakage from the more advanced foreign firm through personnel moving from foreign to local firms bringing their knowledge with them (Cohen 1975: 22; Lall and Streeten 1977: 66–7; Enos 1989: 7).

For foreign investment to be of benefit, it is necessary that such leakages do occur. If foreign firms locate in foreign enclaves, are 100 per cent foreign owned, employ foreign personnel in all technical level positions and only engage the local work force in assembly level operations, then it is likely that the workers will not acquire significant skills and the technology will largely remain in the hands of the multinational firm (Kim 1980: 3; Streeten 1991: 175–6).

Those who believe in an interventionist stance therefore see that there is a strong case for policy makers to ensure that technology transfer takes place and that it does so by the most appropriate means for the level of development of the country concerned. According to this school of thought the state has a role to play in assisting firms in their choice of methods they employ to acquire technology, ensuring that imported technology is at the appropriate level of the stage of development of the industry concerned and most significantly that the technological capability acquired is dispersed throughout the industry.

However the effectiveness of the role played by the state will depend upon the state's capacity to negotiate with foreign firms and channel foreign investment to the areas where it can be of most benefit in technology transfer. To assess the potential benefits to industry requires the input of local business in a coordinated way. At the same time local firms have the potential to transform policy input into obtaining particularistic advantages for themselves at the expense of the state's overall development plans. It is therefore necessary for policy makers to have a degree of insulation and at the same time a cooperative relationship with business for intervention in technology related matters to be effective. On the other hand, those who adopt a more free market approach argue that competitive pressures arising from the pressure of foreign firms in an industry will tend to automatically lead to local firms upgrading their technology and that the state should stay out of this process. Since the early 1980s opinion within the Korean bureaucracy has been divided between these two views as will be seen. This has considerably weakened bureaucratic capacity in relation to this issue.

Avoiding Industry Domination and Adverse Balance of Payments Effects

The issue of ensuring that local firms learn from the advanced technologies, marketing methods and management skills of foreign firms is a major reason for policy makers adopting an interventionist stance. However potential adverse side effects from foreign investment also prompt policy makers to adopt an active role. These arise in part because of the characteristics of foreign investment itself.

Foreign investment tends to occur in industries which are dominated by a handful of large firms in the industrialised countries from which most foreign investment originates. Newfarmer (1983: 166–70) has reviewed a range of studies which have shown that foreign investment in a number of developing countries has taken place in industries in which there are high levels of concentration in the home country leading to the potential for key industries in developing countries to be dominated by a handful of foreign firms. Yoo (1980) has also shown that much of the foreign investment in Korea that occurred in the 1960s and 1970s originated from firms in industries in which there was a high level of concentration in the home country.

The rationale for foreign investment occurring in this way is that highly concentrated industries in the home country are likely to have the most developed ownership advantages which allow them to establish overseas operations competitively. In such oligopolistic industries there is a tendency for firms in the industry to follow market leaders in locating overseas thereby leading to clusters of large firms dominating key industries of the host country (Pfefferman 1991: 211). This can have a number of adverse consequences for economic development in the host state.

First, domination of industry sectors by foreign firms poses a threat to a planned and integrated approach to industrial development by state policy makers (Lall and Streeten 1977: 63). This arises because the priorities of the overall global operations of foreign firms may conflict with the development priorities of the host country (Evans 1979: 276). This is illustrated where the long term control of an industry sector is in the hands of a single foreign firm or a group of foreign firms which form an oligopoly. Should this occur the development of that industry and industries which depend upon it may be directed in the interests of the firm's parent company and its home state rather than in accordance with the development priorities of the host country. A large presence of foreign investment from a single investor country can lead to those firms having such influence in the economy that they are able to collectively pressure the host country either directly or via their home country government for policy measures which may conflict with the developmental priorities of the host country itself (Moran 1977: 95; Lall and Streeten 1977: 175–6). Evans (1985) and Stepan (1978) provide many examples from Latin American and African countries of this conflict of priorities.

Secondly, industry domination by foreign firms has similar adverse effects to local monopolies or oligopolies. These include higher prices and collusive practices which reduce overall welfare in the host country (Hymer 1976: 45; Newfarmer 1983: 169) or excessive product differentiation which wastes scarce resources which could be otherwise be utilised in the development process (Lall and Streeten 1977: 60–2).

In extreme cases, the domination of key industries by foreign firms may lead to dualistic development producing a relatively small modern sector with the vast bulk of the economy and the majority of the population being excluded from the benefits of development (Evans 1979: 288). A significant multinational presence may eventually pose political problems for the government as people rebel against the effects of such uneven development while foreign firms, through their home country government pressure for continued access.

There are both free market and interventionist solutions to the problem of industry domination. Free market solutions in the case of oligopolies or monopolies include the enactment and enforcement of anti trust laws. More interventionist solutions suggest the screening of foreign investment, the imposition of joint venture arrangements and divestiture requirements to guard against these adverse effects. The effectiveness of either solution depends upon the capacity of the state to formulate and implement such measures. As will be argued the Korean state in the 1960s and 1970s adopted an interventionist approach with considerable success. As from 1980, policy makers attempted to change approach towards a more free market stance with less success because elements of the bureaucracy favoured a continued interventionist stance.

Industry domination is not the only adverse consequence which can arise from foreign investment. Uncontrolled foreign investment can also place difficulties in the path of economic development because of its potential to result in a net loss of resources to the host state. This occurs if capital outflows in the form of remission of profits and capital exceed capital inflows (Lall and Streeten 1977: 60; Reuber 1973: 141–9). This capital drain will increase if foreign firms import more than they export particularly if such imports do not save foreign exchange either through providing a cheaper substitute for imports or through providing inputs to domestic firms for use in the production of exports. Foreign firms may be inclined to import rather than purchase locally because of the groups overall international strategy or for price or quality reasons (Lall and Streeten 1977: 179).

The drain on resources can be further accentuated if the loss of state revenue, which occurs through the provision of tax concessions, is not offset by increased investment. Alternatively, if countries do not provide incentives and seek to tax foreign firms there is the potential for those firms to reduce taxable income through transfer pricing practices (Lall and Streeten 1977: 54–6; Hymer 1976: 68) or through the overvaluation of machinery and equipment supplied by their parent company (Moran 1978: 88–9). For all of these reasons, Lall and Streeten (1977), in their study of foreign investment in over 30 countries, concluded that there was little financial benefit to most host states.

The adverse impact of a net loss of resources can be exacerbated if foreign firms borrow their capital locally and then utilise it for the production of consumer goods. In many developing countries consumer goods are only affordable by the elite. If multinational corporations use scarce resources for this form of production it deprives local firms or the state itself of finance necessary for projects which have a higher development priority (Evans 1979: 38; Moran 1978: 93; Hymer 1976: 51).

In order to guard against these possible adverse financial consequences, policy makers again face a choice between market mechanisms and more interventionist policies. Market mechanisms include the overall maintenance of an internationally competitive environment so that distortions in the trading patterns of foreign and local firms alike do not arise. On the other hand, a more interventionist strategy is to impose export minimums on foreign firms and conditions concerning the types of goods that they can produce. Korea opted for the latter strategy in the 1960s and 1970s with considerable success as will be seen in the following chapter.

Conclusion

The alternative approaches that may be taken to foreign direct investment by policy makers in developing countries have their basis in neoclassical and statist theories of development. Neoclassical theorists see a minimalist role for the state as more beneficial to the development process. The state should refrain from interventionist policies which protect either local or foreign invested firms from the rigours of international competition. Protection leads to the risk of government failure in the allocation of resources due to the assumed inevitability of governments succumbing to rent seeking pressures of societal groups in the interests of maintaining power. Consequently policies which seek to restrict foreign investment to certain sectors or impose various performance requirements have the effect of protecting local firms leading to inefficiency and reduced overall community welfare in the form of higher prices and lower rates of growth. On the other hand, the state should also refrain from the provision of costly incentive measures which seek to induce foreign investment because such measures have been shown to be ineffective.

From the point of view of those favouring an interventionist stance, the state has a role to play in managing foreign investment to ensure that the benefits of it are captured by local firms in the interests of economic development. These benefits are not automatic as neoclassical theory tends to assume. While foreign firms have the potential to transfer technology and the international marketing skills necessary for the development process, the state must take an active stance to ensure that this occurs. Further, a laissez faire approach may lead to foreign firms overwhelming their local competition leading to development occurring in their own interest and in the interests of their home countries rather than in the interest of the host state. This conflict of interest arises out of the ownership advantages that multinational firms possess. Multinational firms wish to use these primarily to benefit themselves. Host states wish to see those advantages utilised for enhancing the development of local industry.

The key to the effectiveness of an interventionist strategy depends upon state capacity. In order to effectively employ instruments for the management of foreign investment, states must not only have bureaucracies capable of the formulation and implementation of competent and consistent policies but they must also be insulated in policy matters from societal groups to avoid the rent seeking pressures to which neoclassical theorists refer. The capacity of the state depends therefore on its bureaucratic capacity and its political capacity. The coincidence of these two variables occurring simultaneously and continuing over time explains the ability of top policy makers to achieve their objectives. As will be seen the combination of circumstances which are needed for a high level of state capacity often depend on particular institutional features of the state which are often historically and culturally based.

This chapter has set out the underlying basis for the views held by those advocating a neoclassical approach to foreign investment on the one hand and those advocating an interventionist stance on the other. It is of significance to understand the intricacies of these arguments because top policy markers in Korea in the 1960s and 1970s believed firmly in an interventionist approach. In the early 1980s a new group of key policy makers favoured a more market oriented approach. This resulted in internal conflict within the bureaucracy concerning the direction which should be taken. As will be seen, the cohesiveness of the bureaucracy in terms of its approach played a large role in the meeting of objectives in relation to foreign investment. However, when the bureaucracy became divided in the early 1980s the objectives of top policy matters were not realised. The approach to policy and its acceptance within the bureaucracy generally and society at large has therefore been the key to effective policy outcomes. The factors responsible for the acceptance of an interventionist stance in the 1960s and 1970s are dealt with in detail in Chapter three. However, it is first necessary to turn to the mechanics of that approach and the outcomes which resulted.

2 Foreign Investment during the Park Regime

Introduction

There is considerable agreement among scholars of Korean economic development that up until at least 1980, Korea adopted a highly interventionist stance in relation to foreign investment. Mardon (1990), Clark and Chan (1994, 1995) and Shin (1991) emphasise the role that the state played in channelling foreign investment into selected sectors of the economy. Luedde-Neurath (1984, 1985) and Haggard (1990) emphasise the pervasiveness of the state's intervention with the aim of showing that its approach during the 1960s and 1970s had been anything but liberal. Others (Deyo 1987; Bradshaw Kim and London 1993; Kim E.M. 1992; Evans 1987) emphasise the state's role as a mediator between foreign and local firms in order to ensure that a positive benefit resulted from foreign participation.

This chapter examines Korea's foreign investment policy in the context of the developmental state of the Park era. The state's active role in managing foreign investment led to bureaucrats allocating it to those sectors of the economy that they saw as being priorities for economic development. At the same time measures were taken to ensure that local firms in key infant industries were protected from their more competitive foreign counterparts. Consequently as Koo B.Y. (1984: 21) notes, foreign investment was confined to selected export oriented industries and key import substitution industries. At the same time it was excluded from domestic market oriented industries producing consumer goods and from industries where the domestic market was already well served by local firms. It was also excluded from most service industries except when it could play a complementary role to the manufacturing investment that was taking place.

This chapter shows that the policy approach was effective in that foreign investment contributed to the development of the technological capability of firms in several key Korean industries and provided local firms with international marketing skills. At the same time the potential for foreign investment to have negative side effects was avoided. The approach of the state can also be said to have been effective because it was able to adjust its policy rapidly to accord with changing domestic and international conditions. An ethos therefore developed within the bureaucracy that an interventionist stance can be effective. As will be seen in later chapters, this posed difficulties for policy change and policy outcomes when top policy makers wished to adopt a more market oriented approach.

The first section of this chapter analyses the state's foreign investment policies and their influence on its industrial distribution. The pre and post 1973 periods are considered separately to emphasise the ability of the state to change policy effectively. The second part of this chapter demonstrates the effectiveness of the state's policies in utilising foreign investment as a source of technology and the development of international marketing skills in carefully selected local industries while at the same time avoiding some of the adverse consequences which foreign investment can have on economic development.

Foreign Investment Policies and Industrial Distribution 1960–72

When Park Chung Hee seized power in a military coup in May 1961, Korea's first Foreign Capital Inducement Law had already been in operation for over a year. It had sought to attract foreign investment for the development of industrial, agricultural or fishery resources with the proviso that investment which led to over production in any one sector could be disallowed. The law was initially limited in its application to only those countries with which Korea had treaties of friendship, commerce and navigation. This initially excluded all countries other than the United States. Additionally, it limited profit and capital repatriation to 20 per cent of the original amount of the investment per year. To compensate for these restrictive measures the law provided for a tax holiday of 5 years to approved foreign investments and the elimination of customs duties for imported machinery, equipment and construction materials. The law also provided for 100 per cent foreign ownership. (*FEER* March 11 1960: 525–6).

The Park administration placed the control over foreign investment within the jurisdiction of the Economic Planning Board (EPB) which had been established in 1962 as the principal agency for the formulation of economic development plans and their implementation. This signalled an intention to ensure that foreign investment complemented the overall planned approach to development that had been adopted by the regime. However, due to the political and economic instability at the time as well as continuing concerns about a further invasion from the north, only US

$13 million arrived between 1962 and 1965 (Yang 1972; *FEER* Jan 19 1961: 91; Kim C.J. 1988; Koo 1982).

Changes were made to the Foreign Capital Inducement Law in 1966 to abolish prior restrictions on the level of profit repatriation and to eliminate restrictions which applied in terms of the maximum amount of investment (*FEER* August 18 1966: 305). The provisions allowing for 100 per cent ownership and tax holidays were continued under the law. However a proposal had been made to limit foreign investment from any one country in any single project to a maximum of 30 per cent. While this was defeated as being overly restrictive the administration noted at the time that it would attempt to enforce such a policy by administrative means (*FEER* August 18 1966: 305). This signalled an intention to adopt a joint venture approach to ensure that Korean firms would gain some benefit from the presence of foreign firms.

The 1966 law also specifically provided for each project to be screened by a foreign capital deliberation committee (*FEER* August 18 1966: 305). This allowed the bureaucracy, in consultation with private enterprise, to seek out foreign investment for the large scale industrial infrastructure projects needed to lay the base for further industrial development and for export oriented manufacturing projects which would complement the state's objectives for increased foreign exchange earnings to help finance its industrial development goals.

In 1969–70 a number of policy changes occurred to promote export oriented investment in particular. These included the establishment of an office of investment promotion in the Economic Planning Board (EPB) with extensive powers to facilitate the investment approval process and the establishment in 1970 of a special zone for foreign investors at Masan to provide facilities for export oriented companies to encourage their participation particularly in the electronics and precision machinery industries (*FEER* April 2 1970: 45). However industrial unrest arose in foreign invested firms in the electronics industry in line with a more general movement by Korean workers for increased wages at the time (*FEER* Jan 9 1969: 55). Concerned about the impact that this would have on its plans for foreign investment, the government took the step in 1969 of banning strikes by all workers in foreign firms. After these measures were put in place, there was a significant increase in foreign investment.

Table 2.1 shows its amount and industrial distribution for each year from 1966–72. The industries attracting most foreign investment during the period were textiles and electronics in the export sector and chemicals, petroleum and transport equipment in the import substitution sector.

Table 2.1: Foreign Direct Investment by Industry (1962–72)
(US million dollars)

Industry	1962–65 $	%	1966	1967	1968	1969	1970	1971	1972	1966–72 $	%
Agriculture Forest Fishery	–	–	–	–	1	–	–	–	–	1	6.9
Manufacturing	13	100	14	11	13	12	58	29	58	195	85.9
Fibre/Garment	1	7.7	1	–	1	2	6	4	4	18	7.9
Food	–	–	–	–	–	–	1	–	–	1	0.4
Chemical	6	46.1	12	4	1	3	8	4	4	35	15.4
Petroleum	5	38.5	–	1	2	–	25	2	10	40	17.6
Ceramic	–	–	–	–	4	–	1	7	3	15	6.6
Metals	–	–	–	–	1	1	2	2	2	8	3.5
Machinery	–	–	–	–	–	1	1	2	2	6	2.6
Electric/ Electronic	–	–	1	4	3	5	13	6	6	38	16.7
Transport Equip	–	–	–	–	1	–	–	–	24	25	11.0
Other manufactures	1	7.7	–	2	–	–	1	2	4	9	4.0
Services	–	–	–	–	5	1	8	14	2	30	13.2
Finance	–	–	–	–	3	–	–	–	–	3	1.3
Construction	–	–	–	–	2	1	2	5	1	11	4.8
Electricity generating	–	–	–	–	–	–	5	8	–	13	5.7
Transport/ Storage	–	–	–	–	–	–	–	–	1	1	0.4
Other Services	–	–	–	–	–	–	1	1	–	2	0.9
Total	13	100.0	14	11	19	13	66	43	61	227	100.0

Source: Ministry of Finance 1993: 122, Table 3–17

While initial investments in the electronics industry had been made by well known US firms including Motorola, Fairchild and Signetics (Shin 1991: 52), foreign investment in both the electronics and textiles industries began to be dominated from 1969 by smaller Japanese firms which had begun to lose cost competitiveness in Japan. After the normalisation of relations between Japan and Korea in 1965 Japanese firms no longer faced any impediment to investing in Korea and saw it as the best place to relocate their declining industries (*FEER* Nov 28 1970: 78). From the point of view of Korean policy makers these Japanese companies were able to provide access to export markets, technology and in many cases the physical machinery necessary for operations (Lee C.H. 1980: 31–6; Stoever 1986: 234). Until 1969 investment in these industries had been slight but with the changes in policy in 1969 investment increased rapidly.

The emphasis in the import substitution sector continued to be on the development of industrial infrastructure in oil refineries, petrochemicals, and general chemical industries in which Korea needed the technological skills of foreign firms. In the mid 1960s Gulf Oil had been one of Korea's first investors when it established a joint venture with Korea Oil in the country's first petroleum refinery. Such well known firms as Union Oil and Caltex followed Gulf's earlier lead and established joint ventures with Korean firms in oil refineries. Korea's very first foreign investment had been in the chemical industry in a joint venture between the US based Chemtex company and a Korean company to produce nylon (Koo B.Y. 1982: 15). Other chemical companies followed in chemical fertiliser industries and industrial chemicals (Koo B.Y. 1982: 73). Construction of Korea's first petrochemical complex commenced in the late 1960s and became operational in 1973 (Enos 1984).

In all cases investments were made by technological leaders in their fields demonstrating careful choice by the state of those firms which could bring to Korea the best technology available at the time. Foreign firms in the chemical industry included leading Western companies such as Allied Chemicals, Union Carbide and Dow chemicals and chemical arms of major Japanese combines such as Mitsui, Mitsubishi, C. Itoh and Nichimen (*FEER* May 23 1966: 394).

Simultaneous flows of foreign investment to key export oriented and import substitution industries and the exclusion of it from consumer industries demonstrated the state's capacity to harness foreign investment for developmental purposes. Foreign investment in the electronics and textiles sectors was needed to obtain the international markets to earn the foreign exchange to assist in the development of key industrial infrastructure. Foreign investment was also needed in some of these industrial infrastructure projects as a source of technology. As will be seen foreign investment was only utilised in industries such as chemical and petroleum where the technology could not be obtained by alternate less costly means. This was even more apparent from 1973.

Foreign Investment Policies and Industrial Distribution 1973–78

On January 1 1973, Park Chung Hee announced in his New Year's address that Korea would embark upon a period of heavy and chemical industrialisation. Specific industries to be targeted included shipbuilding, steel, electronics, heavy machinery industries, chemicals and metal industries. In one sense the heavy and chemical industry (HCI) drive as it came to be called was merely an intensification of the industrialisation that Park had engaged upon in the early 1960s. After laying the industrial base with oil refineries, petrochemical plants and general chemical plants, the next step in the process was to attain self sufficiency in the production of steel and metals for the further development of industries such as shipbuilding, industrial machinery and automobiles which would further substitute for imports. In the meantime it was necessary to continue the export drive to earn the foreign exchange to pay for imports.

In 1973, foreign investment policy became more restrictive to ensure a positive contribution by foreign investment to the development of self sufficiency by Korean industry (Kim C.J. 1988: 192; Koo B.Y. 1984: 18). It did this in two main ways. First, the criteria governing approvals for foreign investment were significantly tightened to disallow investment which would compete with Korean companies in overseas export markets or which would divert resources away from the priority areas of the HCI industries. Foreign investment would only be permitted in large scale concerns which were beyond the technological capabilities of Korean industry and in export industries which did not compete with the fledgling Korean export firms. Secondly, the unofficial policy that the EPB had followed in allowing foreign investment predominantly by way of joint venture was formalised in 1973 by allowing majority ownership in only very limited circumstances. In addition a minimum investment amount was prescribed which excluded many of the smaller Japanese firms which had flooded into Korea since 1969 (MOF 1993: 151–5; Stoever 1986: 235).

Chan Jin Kim (1988: 191) notes that prior to the policy change there had been authorisation of investment in some areas which were already adequately served by local firms and in other areas where local firms badly needed infant industry protection. He also points out that there was a perception that some of the larger investments had occurred on terms which were unfavourable to the Korean government. In his view, it was the combination of these circumstances which led to the more restrictive policies being adopted.

The inflows of foreign investment during the period are shown in Table 2.2.

The 1973–74 period needs to be considered separately from the 1975–78 period as far as manufacturing investment is concerned. During 1973–74, it can be seen that the textile and electronics industries dominated investments showing a continuation of the earlier pattern of investment by smaller Japanese firms. It is also noteworthy that this two year period attracted 60 per cent of the overall investment during the whole of the six years.

Table 2.2: Foreign Direct Investment by Industry (1973–78)
(US million dollars)

Industry	1973	1974	1975	1976	1977	1978	1973–78 $	%
Agriculture								
Livestock, Fishery	4	2	1	1	4	1	13	1.8
Mining	–	1	–	–	1	–	2	0.3
Manufacturing	175	128	52	53	80	68	555	78.3
Fibre/Garment	77	37	9	1	2	–	126	17.9
Timber and Paper	1	–	–	–	–	–	1	0.1
Food	–	1	–	1	–	–	2	0.3
Chemical	6	11	12	14	44	31	118	16.7
Medicines	1	2	1	–	–	–	4	0.6
Fertilisers	–	4	7	–	–	–	11	1.5
Petroleum	5	12	3	13	5	9	46	6.6
Ceramic	2	3	0	1	–	–	6	0.9
Metals	12	8	5	6	5	4	39	5.5
Machinery	10	18	5	2	6	7	48	6.8
Electric/Electronic	29	26	9	10	14	11	99	14.1
Transport Equip	2	4	1	4	1	5	17	2.4
Other manufactures	30	3	1	2	1	1	38	5.4
Services	12	32	9	31	18	32	134	19.0
Finance	2	1	1	3	12	10	29	4.1
Construction	1	4	6	2	1	2	16	2.3
Electricity generating	1	2	–	–	–	–	3	0.4
Transport/Storage	1	1	1	–	–	–	3	0.4
Hotels	7	24	1	26	5	20	83	11.8
Total	191	163	62	85	102	101	704	100.0

Source: Ministry of Finance 1993: 180, Table 4–23

By 1975, the change to a more restrictive policy began to take effect. In particular investment in textile industries in which Korean companies had acquired competitiveness fell off rapidly. By way of contrast, the chemical, machinery and electronics sectors, which were three of the six areas targeted under the HCI plan, accounted for nearly

50 per cent of all investment and about 65 per cent of manufacturing investment during 1975–78. All major industry sectors including textiles, electronics, chemicals and machinery showed a significant upsurge in licensing agreements by local Korean companies and existing foreign invested companies with minority ownership (Koo 1982: 106–7) leaving open the conclusion that in accordance with the government's self sufficiency drive licensing was preferred to foreign investment as a source of technology.

The investments that were made in the services industry during the 1973–78 period consisted predominantly of joint ventures between Korean companies and foreign companies for the construction and management of hotels with a view to supplementing export earnings through tourism (Koo 1984: 19). Nearly 60 per cent of the services investment fell into this one area. The other area of the services industry which attracted investment was the construction industry. The aim of the government here was to allow foreign firms to invest in this industry to provide their Korean joint venture partners with the advanced technology needed to enable them to take advantage of the construction boom which occurred in the mid 1970s in the Middle East (Mardon 1991(a)). There was also some limited joint venture investment in merchant banking mainly to facilitate the inflow of foreign investment and other foreign capital.

Japanese investment accounted for nearly 70 per cent of the total investment during the 1973–78 period in contrast to the more equal distribution of investment projects between the US and Japan from 1960–72. It dominated the chemical sector with seven of the eight investments in petrochemicals being by way of joint ventures between Japanese and Korean firms. Koo (1982: 71–80) notes that Japanese firms also accounted for some 77 per cent of the number of foreign firms in the machinery industries and 80 per cent of firms in the electronics industry.

The Effective Management of Foreign Investment in Korea in the 1960s and 1970s

During the 1960s and 1970s the interventionist approach of policy makers was not only evident from the channelling of investment into those industries which development planners had targeted as priorities for development (Koo 1984: 21) but also from its utilisation to ensure positive benefits for the state. State planners achieved this by ensuring that it played a role in technology transfer by limiting it to those industries where technology could not be acquired in any other way and by imposing conditions on foreign firms to ensure that a positive economic benefit resulted from their presence. Throughout the period, loans were preferred as a source of external funding due to the greater control that the state was able to exercise in their allocation. Through these mechanisms, foreign investment worked in conjunction with, rather than against, the development priorities of the state.

Turning first to the general limitation of foreign investment in relation to foreign loans, Table 2.3 sets out both of these external sources of funds for the 1959–80 period. It shows that foreign investment averaged only about 5 per cent of total capital inflow during the period reflecting a clear preference by the EPB for loan capital.

Table 2.3: Foreign Loans and Direct Investment (1959–80)
(Unit: %)

| *Year* | *Loans* | | *Direct* | *Total* | *Amount* |
	Public	*Commercial*	*Investment*		*US $ million*
1959–61	100.0	–	–	100.0	4.4
1962–66	37.5	57.0	5.4	100.0	307.9
1967–71	35.4	59.9	4.3	100.0	2261.8
1972–76	39.9	50.8	9.3	100.0	5988.6
1977	31.8	63.0	5.2	100.0	1970.6
1978	28.7	67.8	3.5	100.0	2848.0
1979	38.3	57.2	4.4	100.0	2833.4
1980	47.5	49.1	3.4	100.0	2800.0
Total	37.8	56.5	5.8	100.0	19015.4

Source: Koo 1982: 28, Table 4
Notes: 1. Loans refer to only those that have a maturity of three years or more
           2. Pubic loans refer to loans induced or guaranteed by government only
              while commercial loans refer to loans induced by private firms

While there was some concern about the level of debt and an attempt made to achieve a better balance between foreign investment and loan capital in the early 1970s (*FEER* April 2 1970: 45; *FEER* November 28 1970: 78), this was short lived partly because policy makers became aware of the adverse effects of foreign investment and therefore imposed more restrictive conditions (Kim C.J. 1988) and partly because it was politically expedient to limit it at that time as will be seen in the following chapter.

The state's role in managing foreign investment also occurred by restricting it to those industries where local firms could benefit most from an association with their foreign counterparts. Consequently it was confined to import substitution industries where Korean firms needed technology and could not acquire it otherwise and to export oriented industries where local firms could benefit from the marketing methods and connections of the foreign firms.

The state relied upon foreign investment as a source of new technology primarily in those industries which could be considered to be apprentice industries. These are industries in which local firms need to work with foreigners in order to understand the production methods and processes required for plant construction, operation and maintenance with a view to learning these techniques for themselves. On the other hand in imitator industries in which local firms can learn how to duplicate products simply by reverse engineering, sending technicians abroad for training or acquiring technology through licensing, foreign investment was not a major source of technology acquisition (Kim Linsu 1980). The state's use of foreign investment as a source of technology for apprentice industries is best seen in the petroleum refining and petrochemical and associated industries.

In the petroleum industry, Korean firms did not have the know how to establish their own oil refinery and associated processes. It is also difficult to acquire such skills in this industry by way of unpacking the technology from the foreign firm's associated technical and management skills (Hill and Johns 1991: 279). It was for this reason that Gulf Oil was invited to establish the Korean petroleum refining industry in conjunction with Korea Oil. This was followed by other joint ventures in the industry. The Korean partners acted very much as apprentices in mastering the techniques of their foreign partners. As Mardon (1991(a): 132–3) notes, by the end of the 1970s, three of the four foreign firms had withdrawn from Korea having passed on their skills in this industry to the local partners. While the reasons for their withdrawal had more to do with their own internal affairs, their stay in Korea had served the state's purpose of imparting to Korean firms the necessary knowledge to operate this industry without further foreign assistance if need be. The only remaining foreign participant in the industry in the early 1980s had further conditions imposed upon it to ensure that its joint venture partner would also be able to take over the venture in due course (Mardon 1991(a): 132–3).

In some parts of the chemical industry, as in the petroleum industry, it is difficult to acquire technology other than through foreign direct investment because many of the products are associated with large international brand names which foreign firms are often reluctant to licence for quality reasons (Hill and Johns 1991: 279). While the Korean government permitted a number of large foreign chemical companies to establish themselves in Korea, it imposed joint venture requirements on them to ensure foreign investment played a major role in the acquisition of technology by Korean firms in this field (Westphal, Kim and Dahlman 1985: 123; Woo 1991: 138–41).

There is other evidence of the state's participation to ensure a positive outcome for Korean firms in this industry. The government played a major role in the planning of the first petrochemical complex, the choice of joint venture partners for the various downstream industries, the negotiation of conditions, the construction of plants and finally the gradual change over of ownership to Korean firms (Enos 1984). Only one product was allocated to each joint venture firm ensuring that foreign firms did not dominate any section of this industry. In the late 1960s foreign participation in the chemical industry was dominated by US and European chemical companies but in the 1970s following the construction of the first petrochemical complex Japanese companies were preferred because of their greater willingness to form joint ventures with Korean companies (Koo 1982: 71).

The state only relied on foreign investment as a primary source of technology in those apprentice industries where the foreign technology could not be acquired in other ways. For example, some other heavy industries did not rely upon foreign investment for their establishment because the necessary technology was able to be acquired by other means. The establishment of the first integrated steel mill by the state owned POSCO corporation did not involve a joint venture. When it was initially proposed in the mid 1960s, some European and US firms had been approached to form a joint venture project with a state owned Korean corporation (*FEER* May 23 1968: 395). However, the final project was undertaken on the basis of licensing and technical contracts with the Japanese Nippon Steel company thereby avoiding the necessity for the greater foreign presence in the industry that US and European firms demanded. Similarly the establishment of the ship building industry also occurred without foreign investment relying instead on licensing (Kim Linsu 1987: 179). Stoever (1986: 236) notes that in the early 1970s a Japanese proposal for foreign investment in a shipyard was turned down by the EPB.

On the other hand in imitator industries where local firms were primarily engaged in copying foreign products, the role for foreign invested firms was primarily one of imparting international marketing skills and earning export income rather than transferring technological capability. The electronics industry is a good example of this, as is the machinery industry.

While there was a relatively large amount of foreign investment in the electronics industry, the weight of opinion is that it played a less significant role than licensing and informal methods of acquisition in the technological development of Korean firms in this area (Westphal, Kim and Dahlman 1985: 123). Linsu Kim's study of the electronics industry examined the process by which some 30 local firms acquired their technological capability. These included firms involved in manufacturing black and white televisions, radios, communication equipment and calculators. He found that the local firms had acquired their technology not primarily through association with foreign joint venture partners but through directly importing details of assembly processes, product specification, production knowledge, technical personnel and parts from their trade contacts overseas. The diffusion of the know how gained occurred through movement of personnel from the initial firms in the industry to newer firms as they established themselves in it. Linsu Kim suggests that the state's policies of protecting the domestic market from foreign competition by limiting foreign firms to producing solely for export was a major factor accounting for the successful establishment of the local industry (Kim Linsu 1980: 258–61). He does not deal with the effect that joint venture partners of foreign electronics firms derived in terms of developing international marketing skills. However, Hong (1994: 21–22) and Koo (1982: 82) tend to suggest that local firms may well have acquired some skills in this area through their association with foreign partners in manufacturing products for their partners' parent companies.

Jo (1977) also conducted a detailed study of two export oriented firms in the electronics industry one of which was a joint venture and the other wholly owned and two domestic market oriented firms in the chemical industry both of which were joint ventures. He concluded that it was in the domestic market oriented joint ventures that the potential for technology transfer was greatest because in those firms some 50–60 per cent of the staff were Koreans engaged in the technical areas and the majority had university education. By way of contrast, in the export oriented firms, he found that only 15 per cent of the Korean staff were technically qualified and only 5 per cent had tertiary education thereby reducing the possibility for transfer of technical skills. This tends to confirm Kim's view that technology transfer from foreign investment in the electronics industry may have been more limited than in other areas.

A study by Bae and Lee (1986) concerning the patterns of development of technological capacity of small and medium companies in the Korean machinery industry also shows the limited role that foreign investment played as a source of technology acquisition. The study examined the processes involved in technology development in more than 12 leading firms in the machinery industry. The authors discovered that foreign technology was absorbed through the copying of foreign products, through the imitation of foreign products from drawings, through the development of new products from drawings and through indigenous research and development. In each case the emphasis was on the efforts of the local firm and assumed a limited role for formal foreign participation. The authors concluded that it was more cost effective for local firms to acquire technology through informal means rather than through joint ventures or licensing.

While Westphal, Kim and Dahlman (1985: 123) note that foreign investment played some role in the development of technological capability in the machinery industries and Amsden and Kim's (1980) study of three major firms in the machinery industry showed that one of these was a joint venture, Koo (1982) notes that licensing played a much greater role. This occurred not only because of the preference of the state for licensing but also because of the peculiarities of the industry which at that time was dominated by a handful of multinational firms. Because of the small scale of the Korean market and because they saw no threat by way of competition from Korean firms, the multinationals were prepared to licence technology to Korean firms rather than establishing operations within the country. This suited Korean planners who in any event saw licensing as preferable to foreign investment for acquiring technology.

The extent to which licensing has been utilised in preference to foreign investment in all industries is clear from Table 2.4 which sets out the number of cases of licensing and foreign investment over the 1960–80 period. In particular the period since 1975 has shown a greater role for licensing in line with the state's more restrictive foreign investment policies.

Table 2.4 shows that the number of cases of licensing of technology increased dramatically from the mid 1970s whereas the number of cases of new foreign investment declined dramatically. This indicates that after relying on foreign investment to gain initial technologies local firms were then able to enter into licensing arrangements in the consolidation phase rather than relying on joint ventures. It also indicates a clear preference by the state for this form of technology acquisition in the interests of independence in technology development.

These results are confirmed by Westphal, Rhee and Purcells' study of 112 exporting firms which examined the sources of technology acquisition by Korean firms (Westphal, Rhee and Purcell 1979). Table 2.5 shows the relative weighting of each source. What is of significance is that foreign affiliates were much less important in product innovation than informal sources such as information from buyers and overseas travel by staff.

Table 2.4: Incidences of Licensing and Foreign Direct Investment (Unit: Number of Cases)

Year	New Direct Investment		New Licensing by foreign firms		New Licensing by local firms
	50% or less	*51% or more*	*50% or less*	*51% or more*	
1962–66	22	15	1	1	31
1967	17	8	3	3	29
1968	25	26	6	3	41
1969	33	15	10	4	47
1970	79	36	20	3	69
1971	71	37	9	1	37
1972	101	88	16	0	37
1973	307	78	22	2	43
1974	156	20	26	5	57
1975	34	11	20	3	76
1976	36	14	31	6	90
1977	44	8	25	2	141
1978	48	5	60	3	233
1979	43	7	53	10	225
1980	34	3	42	10	170
Total	1050	371	344	56	1326

Source: Koo 1982: 64, Table 24

Similarly a study by Lee W.Y. (1989) of the means of technology transfer from small and medium industries in industrialised countries to their counterparts in Korea revealed that in 39 cases identified, there were only 2 cases of technology transfer through a joint venture arrangement. The remainder occurred through licensing agreements.

This brief review of studies lends weight to the observation made earlier that foreign investment was restricted in the interests of self reliance in technology development. This had the advantage of limiting the possible adverse effects of a large multinational presence and encouraged local firms to develop technology themselves. On the other hand it may have precluded access to some technology. On balance Kim and Dahlman suggest that the restrictive policy was beneficial but only because of the high levels of skill and entrepreneurship of local firms (Kim Linsu 1988(b): 256–62; Kim and Dahlaman 1992: 450). This may be attributed to the significant role that the state played in the early provision of research infrastructure through various technology institutes, the emphasis on education generally and the active recruitment of

Koreans who had moved abroad for assistance in the development effort (Kim C.J. 1988: 811–17; Lall 1992: 177–8; Islam and Chowdhury 1993).

Table 2.5: Sources of Information for Product Innovations (%) by Exports in 1976

	Reported Responses (%)
Domestic Sources	
Parent firm	6.2
Sales staff	8.6
Buyer of output	8.6
Other firms	1.6
Total	25.0
Foreign Sources	
Parent firm	1.2
Foreign publications	3.9
Staff overseas travel	19.9
Buyer of output	26.2
Other affiliated firms	16.8
Total	68.0
Unidentifiable	7.0
Total	100.0

Source: Westphal, Rhee and Purcell 1979: 378, Table 8

A number of studies have shown that Korean firms were satisfied that their joint venture and licensing arrangements led to the actual transfer of technology. Jo (1977: 56) notes that in an EPB survey of 86 joint venture firms, 65 per cent of Korean partners gave positive answers to questions concerning the effectiveness of technology transfer. A study by Lee C.H. (1984: 128–31) of technology transfer from Japanese and American companies found that Korean affiliates were satisfied in 76 per cent of the cases that technology had been transferred from their partners. There was no distinction between Japanese and US affiliates. However, Lee did not separate out technology transfer in the case of joint ventures and licensing arrangements making it difficult to tell whether it was more effective in either case.

In addition to the benefits of technology development, policy makers also sought to utilise foreign investment as a learning agent for

Korean firms in international market development (Chu K.I. 1989:1; Haggard and Cheng 1987: 91). Parry (1988: 115) has observed that in view of the Korean government's reluctance to utilise foreign investment as a source of technology due to the availability of other sources, it may have been in the area of international market development that Korean firms obtained the most benefit from their joint venture partners. The effectiveness of the state's policies in this regard can be assessed by an analysis of the role of foreign firms in initiating exports in various industries and the mechanisms which the state adopted to ensure that local firms learnt from the international marketing skills of foreign firms.

The contribution of foreign firms in the initial export performance of Korean industries was extensive. Table 2.6 sets out the percentage of total exports in various industry categories for 1974.

It can be seen that exports of foreign firms accounted for over 80 per cent of total exports in the electronics, metal products and machinery industries. They also played a large role in exports of chemicals and petroleum products. These figures suggest that the early stages of Korea's export success depended on the marketing skills of foreign firms. In time as joint venture partners learnt these skills and as foreign firms withdrew, the marketing skills and contacts remained with their Korean partners.

Table 2.7 shows that during the 1974–78 period the exports of foreign firms continued to constitute a significant percentage of Korea's total exports. On the basis of this evidence and that provided in Table 2.6, it can be concluded that foreign firms provided their joint venture partners with access to international markets in several key industrial sectors.

The specific policy mechanisms that the state employed to ensure that local firms learnt from foreign participation in the relevant industries included joint venture requirements and minium levels of export. The priority that the state placed on joint ventures is evident from Table 2.8. It shows that throughout the entire period from 1968 to 1980, over 80 per cent of all foreign investment occurred by way of joint venture. This provided Korean firms with the opportunity to acquire technology and international marketing skills from their foreign affiliates.

The second mechanism employed by the state to ensure that local firms benefited from the international marketing skills of foreign firms was to ensure that most foreign invested projects exported their product rather than selling it on the domestic market. Jo (1977: 18) points out that in 1974, 89.1 per cent of foreign invested projects exported all or a predominant part of their products. Mardon (1991a: 138) notes that by 1978, 40 per cent were still required to export 100 per cent of their product. Westphal, Rhee and Purcell (1979: 380) note that of the remainder less than half had no export condition imposed upon them.

Table 2.6: Share of Foreign Firms in Exports by Industry (1974)
(Unit: US million dollars)

Industry	Exports by Foreign Firms	Total Exports	Per cent by Foreign Firms
Agriculture, Forestry and Fishery	27.7	299.7	9.2
Mining	1.1	296.4	0.3
Manufacturing			
Foods	4.2	48.9	8.6
Textiles and Apparels	187.6	1536.9	12.2
Lumbar and Wood	6.0	279.5	2.1
Chemicals	222.9	389.3	57.3
Petroleum Products	˙57.0	101.4	56.2
Clay Products	62.3	84.3	73.9
Metals and Metal Products	101.0	120.0	84.2
Machinery and Machine Parts	71.9	77.0	93.4
Electric Machinery and Electronics	420.3	474.2	88.6
Transportation Equipment	0.9	121.1	0.7
Others	79.6	631.7	12.6
Services			
Finance	–	–	–
Construction	0.5	206.2	0.2
Electric Power	–	–	–
Transportation and Storage	–	227.2	–
Hotels and Tourism	–	153.3	–
Others	–	400.6	–
Total	1241.2	5447.7	22.8

Source: Jo 1977: 27, Table 2–4

The desire of Korean firms to acquire international marketing expertise is confirmed by a survey conducted by the Korea Development Institute in 1974 concerning the motivations of local firms entering into joint ventures with foreign companies. The results showed that nearly 50 per cent of the firms surveyed entered into the arrangements for the express purpose of either being able to export to their joint venture partner's parent company or to seek the assistance of their joint venture partner in developing other markets. A further 20 per cent of those surveyed gave their main reason as the acquisition of technology (Jo 1977: 9–10). This confirms what was said earlier concerning the relative importance of international market development as an outcome of the state's policy.

Table 2.7: Exports by Foreign Firms (1974–78)
(Unit: US million dollars; %)

Industry	1974	1975	1976	1977	1978
Total Exports	4253	4791	7283	8795	11420
Foreign Firms	1004	1096	1927	2271	2810
Domestic Firms	3249	3695	5356	6524	8610
Foreign Firms share	23.6	22.9	26.5	25.8	24.6

Source: Koo 1983: 200, Table 4–16

Table 2.8: Cumulative Ownership Distribution of Foreign Firms
(Unit: %)

Year	Minority Owned	Co-owned	Majority Owned	Wholly Owned	Total	No. of Firms
1968	42.5	14.2	24.8	18.6	100.0	113
1970	41.3	22.5	20.3	15.9	100.0	276
1972	35.6	25.1	17.6	21.6	100.0	573
1974	41.4	30.1	13.0	15.5	100.0	1134
1976	41.7	29.9	13.0	15.3	100.0	1229
1978	43.4	29.5	12.7	14.3	100.0	1334
1980	44.2	29.7	12.2	13.9	100.0	1421

Source: Koo 1982: 46, Table 12
Note: Calculated on the basis of the number of firms approved by the government

In addition to ensuring that local firms learnt from the technology and international marketing skills of their foreign partners, the state was able to avoid the adverse side effects of foreign investment. As pointed out earlier foreign investment has the potential to lead to a net capital outflow. Korean policy makers were able to avoid this by limiting foreign investment to key import substitution and export oriented projects and by imposing limits on the level of dividend remission and the amount of local and foreign borrowing. Instead foreign investors were required to bring their capital in with them thereby minimising outflows through interest payments.

Table 2.9 highlights the success of these policies. It shows that during the 1962–80 period foreign investment resulted in a net contribution to the capital account element of the balance of payments for most of the period.

Table 2.9: Direct Balance of Payments Effects by Foreign Firms in Korea (Unit: US million dollars)

Year	Investment Arrivals	Investment Withdrawals	Profit Remissions	Royalties	Net Direct Effect on B of P
1962–66	16.7	–	0.3	0.5	15.8
1967	12.7	–	0.2	0.5	12.0
1968	14.7	–	0.6	0.4	13.7
1969	7.0	0.2	5.5	0.7	0.5
1970	25.3	0.2	8.1	5.1	11.9
1971	36.7	0.6	8.3	3.1	24.7
1972	61.2	2.9	6.7	4.1	47.5
1973	158.4	4.2	15.4	7.0	131.9
1974	162.6	6.1	26.8	7.9	121.7
1975	69.2	5.9	24.0	12.6	26.6
1976	105.6	4.4	37.0	14.8	48.6
1977	102.3	11.0	49.3	30.1	11.9
1978	100.5	11.8	44.1	27.7	16.9
1979	126.0	90.9	54.7	n.a.	n.a.
1980	96.2	90.2	46.8	n.a.	n.a.

Source: Koo 1982: 33, Table 7
Notes: Royalties only refer to those sent by foreign firms

However a net capital contribution to the balance of payments can be offset if foreign firms import more than they export. Korean policy makers were also able to avoid this negative effect as shown in Table 2.10.

The balance of payments effect 1 refers to exports of foreign invested firms less imports. On this basis it appears that imports exceeded exports for the 1974–78 period. However if petroleum is excluded the picture changes from a negative to a positive effect on the current account as a result of the trading activities of foreign firms.

The overall effect of foreign investment on the current account becomes even more favourable if it is assumed that the sales of foreign firms in the domestic market were substitutes for imports. This is shown by the balance of payments effect 2 in Table 2.10. It has been seen that the rigid enforcement of government policy only allowed foreign investment into a selected number of industries. By and large these were either priority industries for export such as textiles or electronics or priority import substitution industries such as chemicals.

Table 2.10: Export and Import Activities of Foreign Firms in Korea (Unit: US million dollars)

	1974	1975	1976	1977	1978
Total Exports by Foreign Firms	1024	1135	1962	2332	2899
Exports excluding petroleum	923	1040	1830	2232	2869
Domestic Sales by Foreign Firms	1853	2406	3144	4209	5731
Sales excluding petroleum	801	1007	1473	2047	3075
Total Imports by Foreign Firms	1932	2253	2966	3476	4172
Imports excluding petroleum	823	909	1311	1439	1889
Balance of Payments Effect 1	–908	–1118	–994	–1144	–1273
excluding petroleum	100	131	519	793	980
Balance of Payments Effect 2	945	1288	2150	3065	4458
excluding petroleum	901	1138	1992	2840	4055

Source: Koo 1982: 35, Table 8
Note: Figures compiled on the basis of a survey of foreign firms conducted by the EPB

Foreign investment was also actively excluded from consumer industries and for domestic market oriented industries other than for the supply of industrial inputs. For example, there was little foreign investment in the agricultural sector or in the food manufacturing industries. Similarly there was little foreign investment in the service industries other than in tourism, construction and finance. The exclusion of foreign investment from domestic market oriented industries assisted in ensuring that the foreign invested projects that did occur either earned foreign exchange from exports or saved it by substituting for imports of intermediate goods. It therefore seems likely that domestic market sales by foreign invested firms did substitute for imports resulting in a favourable balance of payments effect on the current account.

Conclusion

The state limited foreign investment to selected industries during the 1961–79 period. It did so by carefully scrutinising all investment through the Economic Planning Board which also determined those areas which were development priorities for Korean industry generally. Foreign investment was only prominent in industries seen as priorities for export such as textiles and electronics or for import substitution such as chemicals and petroleum refining and to a lesser extent machinery and metals.

The effectiveness of the state's policies has been shown by the net benefit derived by local firms and the economy at large. The policy of the state in utilising foreign investment as a source of technology in only those industries where it could not be acquired in any other way was not only more cost effective but resulted in a positive transfer of technology. This occurred because of the state's joint venture policies and requirements imposed upon foreign investors to transfer their technology to local partners. A more liberal policy may well have provided greater opportunities for technology acquisition. On the other hand it may have resulted in the failure of local industries to develop technological capability because of some of the inherent limitations of foreign investment as a vehicle for the development of technological capability as described in the previous chapter.

In terms of international market development, the state's joint venture policies assisted Korean firms acquire some necessary skills. However the evidence here is less comprehensive than for technology transfer. What can be deduced from that which is available is that joint venture firms made a significant contribution to exports in key industries and that Korean firms specifically entered into these arrangements to acquire international marketing skills. Further in those industries such as electronics which received a large share of foreign investment during this period, Korean firms have now become highly successful in the international marketplace.

The state was also successful in avoiding some of the possible negative effects of foreign investment on the balance of payments. It did so by imposing conditions upon foreign firms which required those firms to either export their production or to substitute for imports. The favourable impact that the interventionist approach had achieved in harnessing foreign investment to the developmental goals of the state made it difficult for those key policy makers who, in the early 1980s, sought to change strategy to a free market approach. This is explored in chapter four. However, it is first necessary to examine the factors which account for the Korean state's ability to effectively channel foreign investment into those industries where it could be of most benefit for the future industrial and economic development of the country. It has already been emphasised in Chapter one that the state's capacity in relation to foreign investment can make the difference between a successful and an unsuccessful interventionist stance. The factors underlying this success therefore need some elaboration.

3 State Capacity and Foreign Investment during the Park Regime

Introduction

This chapter explores the factors underlying the state's capacity for the effective formulation and implementation of foreign investment policy during the era of the Korean developmental state. A detailed discussion of these institutional features of the developmental state is necessary because many of them have survived relatively intact up until the present day and have therefore had a continuing impact upon the ability to bring about effective policy change.

As noted earlier, state capacity rests on both the capacity of the bureaucracy as well as upon the political capacity of the state in relation to its own society and external actors. Bureaucratic capacity implies competence and cohesiveness within the executive branch of the state. Political capacity requires a degree of insulation from societal pressures while at the same time maintaining an embeddedness within society to ensure that policy initiatives are feasible and capable of implementation. External actors can severely constrain policy choice. The degree to which the state is immune from outside pressures can therefore also have a considerable bearing on its policy processes.

In the Korean context bureaucratic capacity arose out of the structural features of the state itself in which the executive branch was dominant. Within the executive branch, economic policy making and coordination was centred in the Economic Planning Board which operated in close consultation with the president's personal economic staff. Structural arrangements between the EPB and other ministries minimised policy conflict resulting in greater cohesiveness (Choi 1991(a); Choi 1991(b): 97; Kim B.W. 1991: 138).

This was reinforced by the dissemination and wide acceptance within the state of a dominant ideology of developmentalism which had as its almost single minded goal the pursuit of economic growth (Paik 1991(a); Kim K.W. 1991; Caiden and Jung 1985). The dominance of this

53

ideology arose out of a strong sense of nationalism emanating from past colonial experiences (Johnson 1989; Onis 1991; Cumings 1987; Koo 1993) and an ever present security threat from the north. In addition, the personal leadership style of Park and his senior political appointees maintained the dominance of the developmental ideology during the term of his administration (Chung C.K. 1986, 1989). In turn the widespread acceptance by bureaucrats of developmental goals and the methods adopted to achieve these were also an important determinant of the state's internal cohesiveness (Kim B.W. 1991(a): 136).

The political capacity of the state in the Korean context has revolved around its ability to resist collective action (Evans 1992; Doner 1992; Haggard 1994; Shafer 1990) through a dual strategy of co-opting the dominant capitalist class into a development coalition (Kim E.M. 1988; Cotton 1994; Moon 1994; Moon and Kim 1995; Weiss 1994) in which the state was the senior partner while at the same time utilising corporatist measures in relation to small business and labour and repressive measures against informal opposition groups to exclude them from direct input into policy change (Deyo 1987, 1989; Lie 1991; Park M.K. 1987; Onis 1991). The dominance of the executive within the formal institutions of the state resulted in relative insulation of the policy making process from indirect societal pressures expressed through the legislative branch (Paik 1991(a): 129; Jung 1991: 73–6). At the same time, the institutions of the state operated in a manner which carried society along with the state's developmental goals. In this sense it was the state's embeddedness in society which determined the effectiveness of its policy initiatives (Evans 1992).

The state is also part of a wider international society (Evans, Rueschemeyer and Skocpol 1985: 350). External actors and external events therefore constrain the state in the policy choices which it is able to make (Haggard 1994: 274; Liddell 1992: 796). In the era of the developmental state, policy makers were able to respond to changes in the international environment without facing significant pressure to adopt positions contrary to the state's developmental goals.

Bureaucratic Capacity and State Structure

The early decisions made by the Park administration relating to the structuring of the executive branch established the institutions which would produce competence and cohesiveness in the policy making process. However, one needs to return to the Japanese colonial period to discover the foundation upon which Park built his bureaucratic state.

When the Japanese colonial administration moved into Korea it found an already highly developed bureaucracy which had established itself during the period of the Yi dynasty as the governing elite (Woo-Cumings 1995: 144–6). However it had become highly factionalised with appointments being made upon patrimonial and nepotistic ties rather than on the original meritocratic practices of the Confucian examination system (Ha T.K. 1993: 73). The landed aristocracy of the Yi period had turned the bureaucratic elite into an instrument for the furtherance of their own class interests (Koo 1993: 232–5; Kohli 1994: 1271). The Japanese were able to make two significant changes. They restored the meritocratic aspects of the bureaucracy and through direct intervention destroyed old factional rivalries. They achieved this largely through structural reform of the bureaucracy to model it on that which existed in Japan and through the intensive training in Japanese bureaucratic practices of those Koreans who were recruited into their administration (Kohli 1994: 1273; Woo-Cumings 1995: 147–51).

However, to place too much emphasis on the structural changes which the Japanese made ignores the significant influence which Japanese ideas about economic development had on the Korean governing elite including Park himself (Kohli 1994: 1286). The Japanese colonial administration in Korea transplanted the fundamentals of the Japanese strategy for economic development through its administrative practices and educational system (Cumings B. 1987: 53). The generation of leaders at the time that Park took power had been subjected to Japanese methods of administration and more importantly the Japanese approach to development in which the state assumed a leadership role in engendering self reliant growth (Cumings B. 1987: 53–5) rather than Anglo-American ideology which assumed a minimalist role for the state as arbiter and regulator (Chang H.J. 1993: 152).

The United States administration and the following Rhee regime had left the structure of the Japanese built bureaucracy largely intact (Cumings B. 1991: 479; Kohli 1994: 1285). The executive branch which the Park regime inherited therefore not only reflected the structural characteristics of the Japanese colonial state but also had a legacy of Japanese developmental strategy. However, it needs to be emphasised that even though the Japanese reforms were crucial to the competence of the bureaucracy that Park inherited and in this respect may have been decisive in the implementation of economic policy in the Park era (Kohli 1994: 1270), the Japanese reforms themselves were built upon a strong tradition of bureaucratic rule (Kim and Bell 1985: 12). Without such a long term tradition of bureaucratic rule the structural reforms instituted by Park may not have resulted in cohesive policy. A highly competent and cohesive bureaucracy takes many years, if not generations, to build (Rueschemeyer and Evans 1985: 59–60; Evans 1992: 156).

The Park regime's major structural reforms were introduced during the period of the Supreme Council for National Reconstruction from 1961–63. One of the most significant of these for economic policy was the establishment of the Economic Planing Board (EPB). It was charged with the functions of economic planning, budget control, evaluation of performance in meeting plan targets and jurisdiction over international economic relations including foreign investment (Kim B.K. 1992: 200; Lim and Kim 1995: 10; Choi B.S. 1991(a): 46–9; Mardon 1990 (b): 460–3). The EPB has also been attributed with having maintained cohesiveness in economic policy formulation and implementation through its role in coordinating the various economic ministries (Haggard 1988:262; Evans 1992: 167; Haggard and Moon 1990: 212; Chang H.J. 1993: 152). The EPB itself was initially a merger of some elements of existing departments with its budget function coming from the Ministry of Finance and its planning function coming from the old Ministry of Reconstruction which had been in existence in the post Korean War years to oversee the reconstruction of Korea with US aid funds (Choi B.S. 1991(a): 26–7). Within a few short years and with the support of the President as its creator, the EPB had assumed preeminence in economic policy making with its ministerial head being elevated to deputy prime minister status dealing directly with the president on economic matters rather than through the Prime Minister (Kim K.H. 1993: 29).

The manner in which the EPB was able to coordinate policy among the various economic ministries is of the most significance as far as economic policy making is concerned (Kim B.W. 1991(a): 136–8). As Choi (1991(a): 52–65) has noted, each of the economic ministries had their own bases of power. The Ministry of Finance (MOF), even though it had lost its budget function, still had control over the banking sector and therefore the allocation of credit and financial incentives while the Ministry of Commerce and Industry (MCI) had direct links with industry through the establishment of industry associations. The task of coordination was therefore a formidable one.

There were several mechanisms used to maintain the EPB's coordinating role and resulting policy cohesiveness. First was the formal requirement for the MCI and MOF to obtain approval from the EPB for increased budgets. However, given their substantial other powers this was not of itself sufficient to achieve policy coordination in matters other than those involving increased expenditure (Choi 1991 (a): 28). A more significant mechanism was the Economic Ministers' Consultation meeting which was the major forum for the resolution of disputes between economic ministries over policy prior to formal endorsement of policy by the Economic Ministers' Conference and subsequent ratification by the State Council. The Deputy Prime Minister for the EPB presided over the Economic Ministers' Consultation meetings and therefore took a lead role in conflict resolution at this level (Choi B.S. 1991(a): 69–76; Choi 1991(b): 98). The EPB's role in conflict resolution was considerably enhanced due to it having no specific societal group as constituents. By way of contrast the MOF and MCI saw their power flowing from their role as the guardians of the banking sector and industry respectively. This necessarily resulted in conflicts from time to time. The lack of a constituency base allowed the EPB to mediate in such disputes (Choi B.S. 1991(a): 349–52).

The maintenance of close links between senior EPB figures and the President's economic secretariat gave the EPB additional weight in its coordinating role (Choi B.S. 1991(a): 30–53; 1991(b): 96–8). As well, the origin of most of the president's chief economic secretaries from within the EPB and their consequent tendency to side with the EPB in disputes over policy assisted in the EPB's dominance in economic policy matters (ibid). The appointment of ex EPB officers as Ministers and Vice Ministers of the other economic ministries including Ministry of Trade and Ministry of Finance also gave the EPB some inside control over the policy initiatives of these ministries (Kim B.K. 1992: 207–10).

The EPB's role in monitoring the performance of various organisations in meeting their targets under the economic plan also gave it significant power over other ministries. This was reinforced through the discussion of the level of achievement of various plan targets at the monthly economic briefing sessions attended by the president. The EPB also developed alliances within the bureaucracy. An alliance between the EPB and the MTI on an expansionary policy to finance the trade promotion effort effectively precluded the powerful Ministry of Finance from pushing for financial reforms which would have advanced the interests of its major constituents, the banks (Kim B.K. 1992: 205–6).

Within the EPB itself cohesiveness was enhanced through the old school tie pattern of recruitment. Kim Byung Kook (1992) has shown that by 1979, 27 out of 29 of the EPB's senior managers were graduates of Seoul National University (SNU). In turn they tended to ensure that subordinates were also SNU graduates (Kim B.K. 1993: 202–4) thereby maintaining a pattern of close linkages between the nation's top universities and its leading bureaucrats (Paik 1991(b): 51). This practice is deeply rooted in the Korean tradition of the scholar-official and has survived to a considerable extent to the present day.

The EPB was also able to utilise the military style command system which Park had established within the bureaucracy to ensure implementation of policy by other ministries. Park's recruitment of ex-military personnel to senior positions considerably assisted cohesiveness in this regard. A number of studies have been undertaken to establish just what role the military played. The first of these was a study by Bark and Lee (1976) in which 175 out of a possible 203 second division public officials were interviewed and biographical data collected from them. Bark and Lee found that at this second most senior level of the Korean civil service administration, some 76 (40 per cent) had a military background. These persons had been recruited through the special recruitment program of the government rather than through the general civil service exam. The authors comment that the purpose of such recruitment was to ensure a high level of military influence in the senior areas of the regime (Bark and Lee 1976: 108).

The civil service itself was not the only area in which military appointments were made. Kwang Won Kim (1993: 54) has shown that nearly 50 per cent of the directorships of government boards (such as in the transport, agriculture and even tax and customs area) were staffed by military elites in the third republic and approximately 35 per cent during the fourth republic. He also shows that military personnel held approximately 40 per cent of the positions of cabinet ministers during the third republic and 30 per cent during the fourth republic. These findings suggest that Park used official positions both as a reward for the past loyalty of military colleagues and to ensure reliability in implementation of policy. However as Chung Kil Chung (1989: 271–2) has noted, Park tended to rely on ex-bureaucrats at Minister and Vice Minister level in the technical areas of economic policy and ex-military personnel in ministries largely concerned with implementation (such as transport, construction and communications). This suggests that while economic policy was formulated by expert technocrats, they were able to rely on military personnel in the line ministries to implement the policies devised.

Loyalty and cohesiveness within the bureaucracy was also enhanced through a pattern of recruitment of bureaucrats from Park's home province of Kyongsan (Paik W.K. 1991(b): 50). Chung Hyun Ro's study in 1979 of a sample of 174 civil servants from first to fifth class (the bureaucratic elite) found that some 31.6 per cent had originated from North and South Kyongsan region (Ro 1993). The disproportionate nature of such recruitment is evident when it is seen that only 6.3 per cent originated from Seoul. Ro contrasts this with the recruitment of senior civil servants in Britain and France where nearly 40 per cent tend to originate from the major capital cities. The regional bias is explained perhaps by Park's own political basis of support which was in Kyongsan.

Cohesiveness relies not only upon loyalty but also upon bureaucratic competence in the sense that poorly conceived or impractical policies are likely to suffer in the implementation phase.

Lower level bureaucrats who are close to social constituents may be less willing to implement such policies. In this respect the Park regime ensured that the political and bureaucratic elites were highly competent. This is reflected in the make up of the cabinet minsters and vice ministers in the economic area as well as in key presidential economic staff and in the EPB. Paik (1991(b): 51) notes that all but 4 of Park's 89 cabinet ministers in the 1963–70 period had a university education and some 97 per cent of bureaucrats above grade 3 level were also university educated. Additionally, bureaucrats were recruited predominantly through the rigorous civil service examination process with the only exception being for those military personnel appointed as mentioned above (Kim K.H. 1993: 30). Even amongst the military personnel, most of those appointed had formal eduction at university level either in Korea or overseas.

The foregoing has shown that there were many mechanisms for ensuring cohesiveness in the senior political and administrative elites and that much of this relied upon the EPB's dominance in the system. However, this should not be taken to mean that the EPB prevailed in policy at all times. The most striking example was the heavy and chemical industry drive announced by Park in 1973. Many senior bureaucrats in the EPB opposed this initiative. This led Park to appoint a special economic secretary with the sole responsibility of overseeing the implementation of the plans (Kim K.W. 1993: 32; Choi 1991(a): 37). It has been suggested that through this mechanism Park was able to simply bypass those elements of the EPB who opposed him (Jeon 1994: 576; Choi 1993: 106).

Ideology, Leadership and Legitimacy

The role of ideology, leadership and the need for legitimacy played a significant role in the Park regime's ability to maintain power and effectively implement policy change. Park's seizure of power from a democratic regime through a military coup in 1961 required him to establish the legitimacy of his regime if he was to maintain power (Koo and Kim 1992: 26; Castells 1992: 56). The cornerstone of Park's strategy in his quest for legitimacy was to choose to give first priority to rapid economic development rather than competing goals such as political or social development (Johnson 1994; Caiden and Jung 1985: 22; Kim B.W. 191(b): 247; Paik 1991(b): 46). This strategy was followed so single mindedly by the regime that the term developmentalism (Kim K.W. 1993: 59) or ideology of economic development (Chung C.K. 1986: 38) has been used to describe the underlying ideology of the bureaucratic and political elite during this period in Korean history.

The widespread acceptance of a developmental ideology can be attributed to the ability of Park's political leadership (Paik 1991(a): 124–5) in channelling nationalism into economic growth. At the time that Park assumed power, there was already a widespread ethos of nationalism which had sprung from a colonial past and the Korean War. Park was able to channel this sense of nationalism in the direction of economic development by appealing to the idea that through economic development Korea could assume self reliance and an improvement in living standards (Park C.H. 1979; Chang H.J. 1993: 152).

The Japanese colonial regime had left a strong legacy of resentment among the Korean population. Unlike the European colonial administrations in much of the rest of Asia, the Japanese colonial regime attempted to absorb Korea into Japan and to that end sought to eliminate much of Korea's traditional social and cultural values through a highly efficient and 'deeply penetrating' administrative network (Kohli 1994: 1273). Also unlike the European colonial administrations, the Japanese believed that such assimilation was possible because of the common cultural roots of Japanese and Korean society (Kim B.K. 1995: 10).

The Park regime was able to channel the resentment built up over the half century of Japanese domination into a drive for development so that Korea would become self reliant and avoid such domination in the future. In a review of his administration published in the year of his assassination, Park attributed the successful development efforts of his administration to the desire of the Korean people to achieve this self reliance. He describes how throughout its history the nation had constantly sought to maintain its independence in the face of invasion from more powerful neighbours. He was of the view that in order to achieve such independence it was necessary to build up the economic strength of the nation (Park C.H. 1979: 21–35).

South Korean nationalism had also been fuelled by the division of the peninsular and the following period of war between North and South. The war left a nation divided and a yearning for reunification (Kim B.K. 1995: 12). The Rhee regime with the support of a similarly ideologically disposed administration in the United States had used the fear of an expansionist and ideologically opposed regime to the North to ruthlessly quell any political moves to give effect to these nationalistic aspirations. However, such a strategy did not guarantee the regime's grip on power and it was overthrown in a student revolution in 1960. The failure of the Rhee regime in economic terms left the way open for Park to channel nationalistic sentiments based on a predominantly anti-communist ideology into an ideology of development. If successful, economic development would not only improve living standards but place South Korea in a position of strength from which to negotiate reunification.

This goal was one which the governing political and bureaucratic elite could readily accept.

The channelling of nationalistic sentiments based upon anti colonial and anti communist sentiments into a dominant developmental ideology was assisted by cultural features within Korean society. Byung Kook Kim (1995: 10–14) argues that traditional Confucian values and ethnic homogeneity have produced in the Korean population a well developed concept of 'nation'. Confucian concepts of the nation as a family with the ruler as its head gives the leader considerable power in setting the course which the nation is to follow (Kim B.K. 1995: 22; Kim Y.K. 1994: 46). Other aspects of traditional Korean values also assisted in the acceptance of Park's developmental ideology in an opposite sense. Paik (1991(b): 125–8) attributes its acceptance to its appearance at a time when traditional approaches to economic growth and distribution had clearly failed in delivering a better lifestyle to the majority of the population. Thus he argues that while people had traditionally held fatalistic views about their lot in life, the jolting experience of Japanese colonial rule led to a willingness to abandon old ideas and accept the possibility of improvement through economic growth.

The foregoing has suggested that leadership, developmental ideology as well as structural features of the administration allowed for cohesiveness in policy processes. However, bureaucratic capacity alone is insufficient to ensure successful policy outcomes. The effectiveness of policy implementation also depends upon the ability of the state to carry society along with its goals. This requires not only relative insulation from societal pressures in policy making processes but also mechanisms to ensure that society will respond to policy when it is made. During the Park era this was achieved through co-opting big business into a development coalition with the state while at the same time excluding other societal groups such as labour from political processes. The objective of this strategy was to ensure that the state would not be distracted by societal demands from the implementation of the goals of its developmental ideology. The mechanisms used by the Park regime in the furtherance of this aim need more detailed consideration.

Executive Dominance and the Exclusion of Societal Input through the National Assembly

Executive dominance has been described as one of the core features of the Korean developmental state (Moon and Kim: 6; Moon and Prasad 1994: 362). It is necessary to explain the roles and interactions of the various formal institutions of the state to see how the executive was able to achieve and maintain its relative autonomy. In doing so, a distinction needs to be drawn between the relatively more democratic period of the Park administration between 1963 and 1972 in which there was greater opportunity for the legislature to influence policy making and the bureaucratic authoritarian regime which ruled between 1972 and 1979. During the latter period, the legislature was excluded from having much input at all due to the alteration of the formal constitutional arrangements under the Yushin system.

When Park Chung Hee seized power in 1961, the National Assembly was the preeminent institution of the state with the president a mere figurehead. One of the first steps taken by Park was to proclaim the National Reconstruction and Emergency Measures which overrode the previous constitution and centred all legislative executive and judicial powers in the Supreme Council of National Reconstruction (Ahn Kil and Kim 1988: 25). Although the national assembly was reinstituted under a new constitution which was passed by a referendum in 1962, the constitution formalised the executive as the most powerful of all state organs and in particular centred power in the president (Han 1986: 121). Most significantly for policy change, the national assembly was given only a limited role in supervising the policy making processes of the executive. Park himself believed that the role of the national assembly was to work in cooperation with the executive rather than acting as a means by which executive power could be checked. He was critical of Western systems of government where legislative institutions played such a role (Park C.H. 1979: 53–4).

The mechanisms used by the Park regime during the 1963–72 period to minimise national assembly input into policy making were several. First, a proportional representation system was introduced pursuant to which parties were allocated additional seats in the assembly according to their electoral performance. When this system was combined with under-representation for urban areas, vote buying and other election irregularities as well as the use of the state apparatus to support the government party in election campaigns (Ahn, Kil and Kim: 26–36; Cotton 1989: 250), it resulted in a favouring of the governing party. Consequently Park's Democratic Republican Party was able to maintain its dominance in the national assembly during the three elections which were held in 1963, 1967 and 1971. Secondly, the president as head of the party exercised considerable control over members of the governing party to pressure them to vote in accordance with the wishes of the executive branch. However, a study of bills presented to the national assembly during the third republic has shown a success rate of only 67 per cent which demonstrates that during this time the governing party was not completely dominated by the executive (Yoon 1991).

The ability of the executive to have bills passed was assisted by the disunity among opposition parties. The disunity of the opposition forces has complex causes. Korean party politics has tended to be centred around the personalities of leading figures resulting in factionalism and rapidly shifting party alliances (Pae 1986: 163; Yang 1994, 1995: 19–24; Cotton 1989: 249). The domination of parties by individuals is facilitated by a lack of willingness to compromise as a part of Korean political culture (Johnson 1989: 9; Johnson 1993: 106; Cotton 1989: 251). Rather than resolving differences of opinion through measures of compromise such as the acceptance of the will of the majority, Korean political parties tend to dissolve and new ones form when serious conflicts arise between major personalities within the party.

The development of a party system has been further impaired by the relationship between assembly representatives and their constituents which has tended towards patrimonialism whereby assemblymen view their primary role as repaying personal favours to their constituents rather than being active in party politics and policy making processes (Yoon 1991: 171 and 198; Kim and Pai 1981: 213). The constitutional arrangements in the third republic which allowed for formal dominance of policy processes by the executive, reinforced these traditional patterns of political behaviour. Thus both structural features of the Korean political system and features of the underlying political culture, resulted in a failure of opposition parties to unite against the ruling party, which itself was dominated by the executive.

The executive's formal power vis a vis the national assembly was considerably strengthened in 1972 with the introduction of the Yushin constitution. The reasons for Park's move to further strengthen the executive included developments in domestic politics and international affairs (Han 1986: 121–4; Koo and Kim 1992: 133). Domestically, Park had narrowly won the 1971 presidential election contested by Kim Dae Jung after a campaign which focused on the earlier amendment of the constitution by Park to allow him to run for a third term of office. The aftermath of the election saw growing opposition to the Park regime, not only in the National assembly but also from labour and student groups. In the international arena, the Park regime was confronted by a US rapprochement with China, a significant US troop withdrawal from South Korea (Jeon 1994: 568) as well as the floating of the US dollar in 1971 which affected Korea's light industry manufactured exports to the US market.

In these changed international circumstances as well as in the face of a continuing security threat from North Korea (Johnson 1994: 77), Park saw the need to revitalise and strengthen Korea not only in terms of the formal structure of government, but also in terms of its society, culture and the economy. He saw that the best way of surviving in a shifting international order was to operate from a position of strength and self reliance rather than dependence on international alliances (Park C.H. 1979: 90–111). Enhanced power for the executive was aimed at ensuring domestic political stability while Korea entered the next phase of building its industrial state through heavy and chemical industry and modernisation of its rural sector through the Saemaul movement (Park C.H. 1979: 48–52).

The power of the national assembly and informal opposition groups was even more constrained by the Yushin system than it had been in the 1960s (Haggard and Moon 1990: 217). The president was no longer directly elected and as well was given the power to appoint one third of the members of the National Assembly. Informal opposition was dealt with through the imposition of press censorship, the abolition of laws preventing arrest without trial, the temporary closure of universities when protests erupted and the arrest of opponents of the new constitution. The Yushin constitution and the continued misuse of state agencies in the elections for the national assembly held in 1973 meant that there was little chance for an opposition victory (Han 1986: 116–19). Yoon (1991) has found that during the fourth republic the possibility for the national assembly having an input into policy making was considerably curtailed. The power of the national assembly to investigate bureaucratic action was abrogated; the number of sitting days of the national assembly fell from an average of 76 days per year in the third republic to only 26 days per year in the fourth republic and the success rate of government bills rose dramatically to 92 per cent indicating an inability of the national assembly to challenge the executive branch and a considerable strengthening of Park's authority over his own party.

Yoon summarises the limited role of the assembly in policy making during the Park and early Chun periods as follows:

> In sum, with regard to the activities ascribed to legislatures...... this study has found that the National assembly has not engaged in a substantial amount of policy making activities. Although the Korean assembly men consider policy making activities, particularly legislative oversight, important and make every effort to perform these activities, there are many impediments, most important of which is the tendency of the executive to limit their function and effectiveness (Yoon 1991: 209).

The dominance of the executive in the policy making process provided a largely unfettered opportunity for it to effect policy change (Kim B.W. 1993: 345). Executive dominance and the cohesiveness resulting from the prevailing developmental ideology reinforced by structural features within the executive branch allowed the state to insulate itself from indirect societal pressures arising from the national assembly. It was also able to insulate itself from the other major societal groups of business and labour.

The Development Coalition

The relationship between the state and the chaebol during the Park period can best be described as a narrowly based development coalition (Cotton 1994: 43; Moon 1994: 146; Haggard 1988: 274) in which the state was the dominant or senior partner (Choi and Lee 1995:39; Kim E.M. 1988: 120; Lee and Lee 1992: 14; MacIntyre 1990:8; Chung C.K. 1986: 41; Shafer 1990: 132; Clifford 1994: 40) thereby minimising pressures by business upon the state and rent seeking by business groups.

Three major features of this relationship need to be addressed in greater detail in order to understand its impact upon policy. First is the issue of how the state established itself in a position of dominance and why it was able to do so. Second, an explanation needs to be offered as to the state's ability to maintain its position of dominance throughout the period of the Park regime. Finally, in order to grasp the significance for policy formulation and implementation, one needs to consider the internal dynamics of the relationship.

The presence of a monolithic and dominant social class impedes the ability of a state to assert its own interest independently of the interests of such a class (Rueschemeyer and Evans 1985: 64). When the Park regime came to power in 1961 it did so neither as an agent for a dominant social class nor owing any political debts to a particular social group. The old landlord class which had permeated the Yi state (Kohli 1994: 1287) had been effectively rendered powerless by the land reforms of the American occupation and a perception by the public that they had collaborated with the Japanese colonial regime. The large business groups that had been fostered by the Japanese colonial regime in the image of their own zaibatsu (Kohli 1194: 1282) had no tradition of forming an independent basis of support and as a result failed to establish any political basis of support during the Rhee regime (Eckert 1993: 97–102). Rather, their relations with that regime were to support it in exchange for the acquisition of Japanese colonial property on generous terms, concessionary finance, priority access to US aid and monopolies in export and import (Jung 1988: 74–75; Jones and Sakong 1980: 59).

The corruption which had characterised the patrimonial ties between big business and the Rhee regime was a precipitating factor in the uprising which led to its replacement by the democratically elected

Chang Myon government in 1960. The Chang Myon government had been given a mandate to stop the corruption which had crept in but internal division concerning what should be done about the chaebol resulted in little concrete action other than the passing of the Illicit Wealth Accumulation Law and the imposition of fines (Kim E.M. 1988: 106).

It was this law which Park used upon coming to power to establish his regime in a position of dominance in relation to the chaebol. He arrested the chaebol leaders and publicly humiliated them parading them through the streets as parasites (Clifford 1994: 39). Charges were brought to have them return their 'illegal' profits to the state. The chaebols' carefully calculated political response was to offer that rather than paying their fines they would donate all of their assets to the state. This placed the Park regime in a difficult position. It had to either take over the running of the chaebols' businesses to keep what little momentum there was in the economy alive or it could arrive at some accommodation with them. Park's counter move was equally as politically calculated. In exchange for the state agreeing to drop all charges, the chaebol would establish enterprises as directed by the state with funds provided by the state and relinquish their controlling shares in the banking institutions (Jung 1988). The enterprises to be established by the chaebol were in industries seen as economic priorities by the regime and included cement, electrical machinery, iron and steel, fertiliser and refrigeration (Kim E.M. 1988: 107). It was announced publicly that these factories would then be donated to the state.

While no such transfer ever occurred and in many cases the proposed facilities were never even built, the Park regime had achieved a measure of legitimacy through leading the public to believe that it was now firmly in control of the chaebol (Kim E.M. 1988: 107). At the same time, it had established a working relationship with them by co-opting them into a development coalition which was very much upon terms directed by the state.

The success of the Park regime in establishing itself in a position of dominance, does not explain how it was able to maintain this in the light of the increased wealth of the chaebol resulting from economic growth and the potential political power which flowed from this. The explanation for the maintenance of the state's dominance in the business government relationship, can in part be traced to the instruments of control over business which the Park regime had at its disposal. Control over finance has been seen by many as a key instrument used by the state to control the chaebol (Mardon 1991(b): 466; Koo and Kim 1992; Jones and Sakong 1980; Jung 1988: 76) Through its control over both the domestic banking system and over foreign capital, the state was able to allocate finance to priority areas in accordance with the performance of business.

The ready access to state guaranteed finance led to the chaebol adopting a philosophy of expansionism through sales maximisation (Janelli 1993: 91–5; Jung 1988: 79) with little regard for the company's level of indebtedness. This in turn provided the state with an instrument of last resort. If any chaebol failed to follow government directives further credit could be cut off leading to bankruptcy. This was the fate of the Yolsan corporation in 1979 and the Kukje corporation in the Chun period (Mardon 1991(b): 476–7).

The control over finance was supported with a range of other controls over economic activity including an extensive system of licensing for all forms of new business, a system of price controls and a discretionary taxation law (MacIntyre 1990: 11; Mardon 1991(b): 471–2). The combination of all of these measures gave the chaebol little flexibility for expanding into new areas of economic activity without state approval even if they could finance them through group earnings.

Although the state possessed significant features of control, business was not without some bargaining power of its own. The state relied on business and particularly the large business groups for economic growth and hence the very survival of the regime (Haggard 1994: 275, 279 and 294). As well in a more direct sense the state relied upon the chaebol in funding election campaigns through the extraction of various quasi taxes in exchange for the granting of permission to engage in various lines of business. While this gave the chaebol some bargaining power in relation to particular issues at particular times (Doner 1992), the state had the means to prevail in any difference of opinion (Clifford 1994: 64; Chung C.K. 1986: 41).

There is also some evidence of voluntary acquiescence by big business to a position of state dominance and leadership. Traditional Confucian principles attach great importance to the ruler's direction over all aspects of social activity and in this sense the state was able to appeal to cultural values and its developmental ideology to maintain its leadership role (Kim Y.H. 1994: 46; Maratello 1991: 85). Janelli's study (1993: 110–15) of the internal management of a Korean chaebol shows how business groups utilised a traditional respect for state leadership to reinforce their own leadership position within the company by tying company goals to broader state goals.

A position of dominance is not sufficient to call forth the extraordinary performance which led to sustained economic growth. As a number of observers have noted, business cannot be commanded to perform, it must be persuaded to do so (Kim K.H. 1993: 37; Moon and Prasad 1994: 363). The key to effective persuasion lay in the cohesiveness of the relationship. In the Park era there were a number of both formal and informal mechanisms which existed to maintain the cohesiveness of the development coalition.

The major formal mechanisms used by the state in its relationship with the business sector was a corporatist system of controls through industry associations (Park M.K. 1987). The industry associations were the means by which the state was able to relay its policy initiatives to the individual firm level. At the same time, through state appointment of the leadership of each association, the state was able to monitor compliance with state directives. The complex licensing system for business operations was dependent upon one's membership of the relevant industry association. Failure to belong to the association or failure to comply with government directives meant removal of an operating licence. In addition to the state dominated corporatist system of control, larger corporations also had access to the state through other formal and informal mechanisms. However, for small business these opportunities were limited resulting in the relative exclusion of this sector from participation in policy processes.

Additional formal mechanisms available to the chaebol included monthly meetings attended by both senior government officials including the president and senior business leaders to review economic trends. As well there were formal meetings presided over by the President between major exporters and relevant government personnel to deal specifically with export performance (Weiss 1994: 100; Kim K.H. 1993: 31; Chung C.K. 1989: 277; Choi B.S. 1991(a) and (b); Shin 1991: 57).

These formal mechanisms were backed up by significant informal contact. The extent of these informal contacts have led some observers to characterise the business government relationship as a network relationship (Shin 1991; Yeom 1994) or as similar to the internal operations of a large corporation (Lee C.H. 1992). The network approach is grounded in the cultural practices and traditions of social relations in Korea. Social relations depend to a considerable extent on a complex social hierarchy with one's position in the hierarchy determined by the network connections one has made through such means as old school ties, regional affiliations, kinship groups, and associations formed through past military service. The existence of such cultural practices in part explains the lack of development of more formal institutional means through which businessmen relate to the state. In turn this means that business must continue to rely upon such networks for access to the policy making and implementation process.

Shin (1991: 55) suggests that it is these network relations which have extended the influence of the state into the 'main arteries' of the nation's economy. He notes that in the Park era the state actively encouraged network relations through a policy environment which required a means of monitoring conformity by business with state objectives, through keeping the business sector dependent on the state for resources and through the practice of appointing retiring government officials to key industry associations. The advantages of networks in securing successful policy outcomes has been attributed to the access to information provided to the state through such linkages in policy formulation as well as the monitoring mechanisms which networks provide to assist with policy implementation (Yeom 1994: 253–79). On the other hand the disadvantages with excessive reliance on this method of business government interaction lies in the opportunities that it provides for rent seeking by business and predation by the state. The limiting of direct network ties predominantly to the chaebol (Chang H.J. 1993: 147) and the features of corporate coherence described earlier minimised rent seeking during the Park era (Evans 1992: 144). However, such practices increased during the 1970s in line with the selective promotional policies which accompanied the HCI drove. In response to such practices, the state undertook two major anti-corruption purges of the civil service during the 1976–77 period (Jun 1985: 62–8).

The dynamics of the business government relationship described above assisted considerably in both the formulation and implementation of policies. In the formulation stage the state had the advantage of business input but due to its position of dominance faced few constraints as to the direction of major policy initiatives. At the implementation stage the close network ties between business and government provided the state with the mechanisms to persuade rather than command resulting in more cohesive policy outcomes (Shin 1991: 55). The nature of the relationship has led some to describe it as embedded autonomy in the sense that the state retained some political independence in its policy processes but at the same time formed those policies within the context of sound business advice (Evans 1992). Weiss (1994: 91) argues that it was the dynamics of the business government relationship which were absolutely crucial to cohesive policy outcomes. However, neither embeddedness nor cohesiveness are appropriate to describe the state's relationship with the other main social group, the working class.

Labour in the Developmental State

While interests representing big business were coopted by the state in policy formulation and implementation and thereby contained in this way, interests representing labour were largely excluded. The exclusion of labour from policy processes raises three further issues. These are the rationale for excluding labour, why it was possible for the state to adopt and maintain this stance and the mechanisms by which it achieved this.

The rationale for excluding labour from policy making is linked to the prevailing developmental ideology. An ideology of developmentalism which has economic growth as its single minded pursuit necessarily conflicts with an ideology of welfarism which has as its first priority the direct improvement of living standards (Johnson 1989: 5). The conflict arises over the priority for the distribution of the gains from economic growth. Working class political movements are oriented towards utilising political power to capture directly as much of the gain as possible for labour by seeking to make improvements in wages and conditions a precondition for continued economic growth. Business interests however see the first priority as the use of the gains for further investment and distribution of the gains to labour as a secondary consideration (Choi J.J. 1989: 266). If the state allows the existence of a politically oriented labour movement, this can pose a threat to the stability which the capitalist class claims as being necessary for long term planning for investment for economic growth. Because of the Korean state's preference for a strategy of growth over distribution and because of its alliance with big business, the state actively worked against the formation of a politically oriented labour movement during the 1960s and more so during the 1970s.

The existence of a politically powerful labour movement may also in the longer term, destabilise the development coalition to such a degree, that old institutional configurations arraigned against labour disappear and are replaced by an institutional configuration, which gives interests representing labour the possibility of taking power. A politically oriented labour movement would have constituted a direct threat to the maintenance of power by the Park regime and this heightened the regime's resolve to contain political activities of not only labour but other political forces which might align with labour including students and the formal opposition (Han 1986; Im 1987).

Turning to the issue of the state's ability to exclude labour it is useful to first look to historical factors. A number of authors suggest that at the time the Park regime took power there was no unified and organised working class movement (Haggard 1988: 263; Choi J.J. 1989: 313). This in turn can be traced to the active repression of the labour movement during the Japanese colonial administration and in particular during the 1930s when Korean labour was harnessed towards the Japanese war effort (Kohli 1994: 1283; Cumings 1991: 494; Deyo 1989(a): 118). Despite the emergence during the 1940s of several pro working class political parties with wide popular appeal (Kim B.K. 1995: 21), the American occupying forces favoured the stridently anti communist and anti labour policies of the supporters of Sygman Rhee

(Deyo, Haggard and Koo 1989: 44). The Rhee regime maintained an active policy of repressing the labour movement due to its earlier link with the communist party and established the Federation of Korean Trade Unions (FKTU) as a corporatist means of control over plant level labour unions (Deyo 1989(a): 119; Deyo Haggard and Koo 1989: 44).

The democratic interlude of the Chang Myon regime did not provide sufficient space for labour to form a unified and enduring political movement. Although there was rapid growth in the number of unions at this time, internal divisions precluded an enduring politically oriented labour movement (Deyo 1989(a): 120) so that when the Park military junta seized power, they did not have to confront a cohesive and well orchestrated force. In this regard the weakness of the labour movement aligns with the weakness of other societal forces leaving no dominant social classes and a power vacuum in society which the state was ready and willing to fill. The striking difference between business and labour as societal groups was that the labour movement had been tied historically to an enemy communist ideology while the capitalist class, although as politically underdeveloped as labour, were able to more readily identify with the developmental ideology of the state.

The early pattern of industrialisation embarked upon by the Park regime was also not conducive to the formation of a politically powerful labour force. The export oriented labour intensive industrialisation embarked upon in the 1960s relied predominantly on the recruitment of surplus labour from agricultural areas which had no tradition of a labour movement (Koo H. 1990: 673). The labour force in the new industries consisted predominantly of young women who engaged in employment often on a temporary basis in small scale, geographically dispersed production units with a view to supplement the family's rural income (Koo H. 1987: 156). Shafer (1990: 135) notes that 70–75 per cent of the employment growth in Korea in the 1960s occurred in these labour intensive industries. The small scale of their production workshops, temporary nature of employment, geographic disbursement and low skill level militated against the effective formation of a labour movement in this pattern of industrialisation (Shafer 1990: 134).

This contrasts with the situation that developed in the 1970s as Korea began its heavy and chemical industry drive. The majority of workers in these industries tended to be males and the establishments were large scale providing greater possibilities for the formation of unions which could take effective action (Lie 1991: 507). It has been noted that the majority of strikes came from the heavy industry area thereby verifying the greater potential of unions in these industries to mount a political challenge to the regime. It was this greater challenge which led to a gradual tightening of the mechanisms which the state used to control the political aspirations of the labour movement.

The third issue raised above concerns the mechanisms for the control of the labour movement. The Labour Union Law was amended in 1963 setting out the procedural requirements for establishing a union and its dissolution, providing for union operation and leadership requirements and most significantly barring unions from all political activity (Choi J.J. 1989: 307–9). The institutional mechanisms used to enforce this law were that there would be only one union per enterprise which was affiliated with a single national industry wide union which in turn was affiliated with the Federation of Korean Trade Unions (FKTU) (Choi J.J. 1989: 307–9). This structure allowed the state through the Ministry of Labour to strictly monitor compliance with the law as well as moderating demands for wage increases (Deyo 1987: 185). The aim of this structure was therefore not as a vehicle for channelling workers' input into policy making but rather as a system of maintaining control over any political movements which the union movement might form. The state also relied upon more covert mechanisms to ensure that various aspects of the law were complied with. These included the use of KCIA officers in detecting potential opposition through undercover operations in potentially troublesome work places and more directly through the use of the police in forcibly breaking up strikes (Mardon 1991(b): 481).

By the late 1960s Korea was experiencing labour shortages and as a result workers began to demand higher wages (Jeon 1994: 568). After a period of increasing industrial unrest in the late 1960s and early 1970s, the Park regime amended the labour laws to prohibit the right to strike and to impose compulsory arbitration by the state over collective bargaining (Choi J.J. 1989: 307–9). The introduction of the Yushin system in 1972 was accompanied by the increasing use of force against political opposition from the labour movement as well as from the increasingly large sections of society who began to resent their total exclusion from political processes. There are a number of reasons for the change in labour policy including the threat that unfettered collective bargaining would have posed to economic growth through escalating costs (Choi J.J. 1989: 310) but more importantly because success in collective bargaining issues at the work place level may have resulted in the potential for greater effectiveness in wider political issues.

Although these factors explain the effectiveness of the state in excluding labour from policy making processes, one needs to go further to show why despite such exclusion, the labour force remained motivated enough to contribute significantly to the rapid economic growth which occurred. While the sheer necessity of earning a living and the fear of having that taken away is a strong motivating force for labour compliance, it is not always sufficient to ensure a standard of performance which will lead to the productivity gains necessary for rapid economic growth. The Park regime used two mechanisms to attempt to bring forth the best efforts of workers.

The first of these was reasonably careful attention to conditions (Chung C.K. 1986: 36). While collective bargaining was controlled by the state, it did lead to increases in wages. Other benefits were provided for workers as well through the amendments of the Labour Standards Law and the enactment of other laws to confer benefits on the working class. During the 1970s, employers were compelled to look after medical insurance for employees, a worker's compensation scheme was introduced and the tax laws were amend to reduce the taxation burden on salary earners (Choi J.J. 1989: 258–63). These improvements in conditions should not however, be seen as due simply to successful bargaining by the labour force through the FKTU but rather that the state realised the political necessity of keeping the work force motivated through better conditions to compensate for the exclusion of labour from the political scene. However, the attention of the state to the steady improvement of conditions during the industrialisation process was only partially successful. The dominant state ideology which favoured the capitalist class as well as the dynamics of the development coalition placed constraints upon the state in the strict enforcement of improvements in conditions and as Choi (1989: 263) notes the enforcement of improvements in conditions was uneven. This in turn led to demands by labour for greater political control over their conditions rather than dependence upon a state system which was weighted heavily against them.

The Park regime attempted to forestall these demands for political participation through attempts to include labour in the rhetoric of its development ideology. Park often referred to the work force as the foot soldiers in the war against poverty (Chang H.J. 1993: 152; Park C.H. 1979) and exhorted the workforce to perform with slogans such as 'my prosperity' which emphasised the personal benefits of economic growth (Kim Y.H. 1994: 48). More substantive attempts to reach the masses were needed when the regime clamped down upon workers' rights in the early 1970s. As a part of the overall revitalisation of the nation envisaged by the Yushin system, Park instituted the village samaeul movement for the improvement of agriculture. This was followed with a factory samaeul movement which had the aim of improving productivity and labour management relations in the workplace and as such appeared to be an attempt to install a system of industrial cooperation rather than confrontation.

However, as Johnson (1994: 77) has said, the attempt to motivate the work force with ideology was also an attempt by the regime to convince them that their situation was a result of anything other than their position in relation to the state. Such an attempt cannot hope to forestall forever a challenge to the power of an exclusionist regime. While the Park regime's attention to improvements in some conditions was partially successful, it could not avoid the inevitable trade off between the competing interests of big business and labour. From the point of view of labour this trade off was too frequently made in favour of the capitalist partners in the development coalition. By 1978, a loose alliance of labour, student and church groups opposed to the regime had been formed. The increasing protests by these opposition groups were supported by the formal opposition in the national assembly. This led to a dispute within the top echelons of the state as to how to deal with it. The outcome was the assassination of Park by his chief security adviser on October 26, 1979.

It can be concluded that the exclusion of labour from political processes in the Park era was accomplished by a highly developed state corporatist system. At the same time an attempt was made to coopt the working class into the development effort through some improvements in conditions and an appeal to ideology with the promise of a better life in the future. As will be seen in the following chapters, this strategy became untenable in the 1980s with the state resorting to increasingly repressive measures to contain labour's political ambitions as well as to restrain wage increases.

The State and Foreign Investment Policy

Foreign Investment policy illustrates how the dual features of bureaucratic capacity and political capacity in the Park era led to policy outcomes which aligned with the state's objectives. The state's bureaucratic capacity ensured cohesiveness in formulation and implementation processes while the state's political capacity restricted the ability of either big business or the labour movement to distract the state from the achievement of its policy goals.

In 1963, the Park regime placed foreign investment policy within the jurisdiction of the EPB. It has been seen that the EPB figured prominently in coordinating economic policy and had the necessary bureaucratic power to prevail over competing views of the other economic ministries should disputes arise. The EPB's jurisdiction over the state's planning processes also allowed foreign investment to be allocated to those industries where it could best be utilised in achieving the state's developmental goals.

The bureaucracy was able to coopt big business in its plans for the use of foreign investment. The Federation of Korean Industries (FKI) assisted in seeking out suitable foreign partners for Korean firms (Park M.K. 1987). Business was represented on the foreign capital inducement committee established under the auspices of the EPB as the ultimate formal body to approve investment. The consultation process between the EPB and relevant ministries as well as between these ministries and their constituent organisations ensured that the investment that was approved would not adversely affect the interests of Korean industry (USITC 1989: D4). Close network ties between business and bureaucracy resulted in the careful selection of those investment projects which would confer the most benefit on Korean firms, as discussed in detail in the previous chapter. At the same time, the jurisdiction of the EPB over the approval process, its lack of a natural constituency and its ability to override other ministries minimised rent seeking.

In 1965 and 1966, the state substantially revised its foreign investment laws in an attempt to attract investment to assist it with the export oriented industrialisation plan upon which it had embarked in the mid 1960s upon advice from the United States and the International Monetary Fund (Wade 1992: 314). This revision to foreign investment laws had also been preceded by a treaty which had normalised relations with Japan. The treaty had been opposed by student groups, some intellectuals and the opposition. As Yoon (1991: 36) has pointed out, although the formal opposition were united in opposing the treaty, they were unable to agree on the tactics necessary to attempt to defeat it. The result was that despite continuing protests the bill and the revision to the foreign capital inducement law were passed demonstrating the executive's ability at the time to override significant formal and informal societal opposition to policy change.

Informal opposition to the foreign investment law continued during the latter part of the 1960s. It was seen as a vehicle for a new period of Japanese neo colonialism. Statements by various minsters in the Japanese parliament supporting the idea of an economic union between Japan and Korea in which Korea would take over Japan's uncompetitive labour intensive industries further inflamed the opposition to the law within Korea (MacCormack and Gittings 1977: 132–3). However, far from capitulating to opposition demands, the Park government embarked upon policy measures to further encourage Japanese investment. In 1969, a one stop shop was established to ease the administrative difficulties faced by foreign investors and in 1970 the Masan special economic zone provided investors with cheap industrial facilities. To further encourage investors, the labour laws were revised to prohibit strikes in foreign invested firms.

The changes to the foreign investment laws in 1973 were designed to limit foreign investment to cases where it could be shown that it would lead to new export markets or provide essential technology. The nature and timing of these changes in policy coincided with Park's announcement that his regime would embark upon a period of heavy and chemical industrialisation. It is apparent that the changes to the foreign investment laws were designed to ensure that foreign capital would be harnessed in this new goal of the state. It also did not pose too great a risk of repercussions from major trading partners because many other countries in Asia such as Indonesia, Malaysia and Thailand also imposed joint ventures requirements on foreign investors in the early 1970s. At the same time Park's view of self reliant development required that foreign capital should not dominate any of the new heavy and chemical industries but should take a role only as a joint venture partner providing the technology and skills which Korean companies lacked.

While the decision by the Park administration to adopt a more restrictive foreign investment policy in 1973 has been explained as resulting from an awareness of the possible adverse effects that accompany it (Kim C.J. 1988: 191–2), continuing societal opposition to it may also have been a significant factor. The opposition to foreign investment was influenced by its origin in the two countries which had occupied Korea in the recent past—the US and Japan. The surge in investment applications which had occurred in the early 1970s from Japanese firms in particular appeared to provide supporting evidence to those who had argued in the mid 1960s that the normalisation of relations with Japan was the first step in a new form of colonisation (Sunoo 1978: 333). The Masan special economic zone was seen as the beachhead for the next wave of Japanese invasion in the form of foreign investment (*FEER* Aug 1 1975: 54; Amirahmadi 1989: 174).

The 1973 tightening up of foreign investment policy can therefore be explained in part by the mounting opposition to it that policy makers had continued to face since the mid 1960s. As has been noted, Park initially refused to respond. However, in the interests of gaining public support for his aim of self reliance in the heavy and chemical industries, the regime may have felt it necessary for the sake of consistency to stem the tide of Japanese investment that was widely perceived as drawing Korea into a dependent relationship with Japan.

This illustrates an important point in relation to the Park regime. While formal and informal opposition groups were increasingly constrained in their direct input into policy processes through institutional means, this did not mean that the governing elite was impervious to all forms of societal pressure. Because of its increased need to maintain legitimacy after the promulgation of the Yushin constitution, it was necessary for the ruling elite to take account of significant societal concerns. Foreign investment was one of these concerns. As has been seen, labour conditions were another. One of the defining features of the Park regime was that while it needed to respond to these concerns, the manner in which it did so was largely free from direct societal influence and was effective because of the internal cohesiveness of the bureaucratic agencies of the state.

The Park regime's ability to respond to internal societal concerns was assisted by the lack of external constraints on the options which the state might pursue. It is noteworthy that the Park regime faced no significant pressure from external actors with regard to its decision to restrict foreign investment. As has been shown, Japan and the US were the major investors in Korea at the time. As a front line state, Korea was an important part of the Western alliance system. It was able to use this geopolitical situation to insulate itself to a considerable degree from external pressures on domestic policy issues.

Cotton (1994:45) has noted that during the Park era Korea faced no US pressure against unfair trade practices and a similar situation could be said to have been the case for foreign investment. Rather, a number of authors argue that the US took positive steps to reinforce the policies of the Park regime (Ogle 1990; Caiden and Jung 1985: 24). Others see changes in US policy in the early 1970s as providing the Park regime with a ready means to convince the population that a greater push towards self reliance was necessary. (Woo 1991: 182–3; Koo and Kim 1992: 133). From both of these points of view, the effect of US foreign policy at the time was to support, rather than detract from, the policy directions of the Park administration. This contrasts markedly with the situation which existed from the mid 1980s in the changed geopolitical circumstances as will be seen.

Conclusion

The state's capacity to devise and implement a foreign investment policy which led to favourable outcomes for the development process was closely tied to the institutional features of the state itself. These included a competent bureaucracy whose cohesiveness depended upon the dominance of a single agency, the EPB, which worked closely in conjunction with the chief policy makers in the presidential office and with business groups in both the formulation and implementation of economic policy matters.

At the same time this preeminent policy making body was able to resist rent seeking pressures from big business groups as well as internal competitive pressures from other ministries. In addition to the many formal and informal mechanisms which fostered the coordinating role of the EPB, the prevailing developmental ideology which was widely accepted by state institutions and business groups alike, assisted in insulating its policy processes. The location of the jurisdiction over foreign investment within the EPB was a major factor accounting for the state's capacity in relation to this issue.

The state's autonomy in relation to general societal pressures through its exclusion of the labour movement and the national assembly from most policy matters meant that there was little distraction from the use of policy measures to pursue the state's goals of harnessing foreign investment in pursuit of self reliant growth. The particular circumstances of the international political and economic environment that prevailed during the period minimised the pressure that major actors such as the United States were prepared to apply to Korea on behalf of US business interests.

At the same time, the Park regime needed to maintain legitimacy. Park's leadership style, the state's internal configuration and the demonstrated fulfilment of development goals assisted considerably in this regard. While the regime needed to respond to societal concerns, its insulation from societal groups and its internal cohesiveness provided freedom in policy choice and effectiveness in policy outcomes.

The institutional arrangements of Park's developmental state were built upon a strong sense of nationalism and a long standing bureaucratic tradition. It has been necessary to set out these institutional arrangements in some detail because, as will be seen, just as it is impossible to construct such arrangements quickly, it is equally difficult to dismantle them in the short term.

4 Chun Doo Hwan and Attempted Foreign Investment Policy Reform

Introduction

It has been shown in the previous two chapters that during the Park era, the institutional features of the developmental state allowed for an effective interventionist stance to be taken to foreign investment. This chapter suggests that beginning in 1979 a fundamental difference of view emerged within the Korean state between those top policy makers who advocated a free market approach and those working level bureaucrats who, having been schooled in the policies of intervention, were unwilling to relinquish their managing role over economic activity. This meant that the internal cohesiveness of the bureaucracy began to decline. The removal of the EPB's jurisdiction over foreign investment along with weaker leadership exacerbated this trend.

However the difference of approach within the bureaucracy has been at the core of the difficulties for foreign investment policy reform since 1980. It also partly explains its lack of effectiveness in achieving the objectives set by top policy makers in the state. As has been seen, the primary objective of a free market approach is to remove restrictions on foreign investment to allow the market to be the determinant of its volume and industrial distribution.

Since 1980 the debate between free market advocates and interventionists has hinged around two issues. The first concerned the extent to which domestic industries should continue to be protected from foreign competition. This issue dominated the debate until the early 1990s. It initially arose because of the need for industrial restructuring in the late 1970s. Those favouring a change to a market oriented approach believed foreign investment could play a role in industrial restructuring through promoting competition (Lee K.U. 1986: 10–11; Park and Kim 1992: 4). If foreign firms were attracted to a particular sector they would compete with domestic firms thereby eliminating excess capacity in that sector and making the industry more efficient overall. Consequently it

79

was necessary to open up the sectors in which foreign investment was allowed, permit foreign firms to utilise their ownership advantages through allowing 100 per cent foreign ownership and overhaul the screening process to prevent the bureaucracy refusing an investment because of fear of the damage it might do to local firms. At the same time the costly provision of universal tax incentives should cease.

Opposed to this view was the traditional view of the government bureaucracy. This view was based on the premise that infant industries need to be protected until they reach a level where they can compete with international firms at which time protection should be removed (Amsden 1989; Biggs and Levy 1991; Kuznets 1994; Chang H.J. 1993). To allow foreign competition into areas of infant industry or industries that were not yet internationally competitive posed all the dangers of domination of core industries by foreign firms referred to earlier. For this reason the working level bureaucrats opposed foreign investment which was seen to be a threat to those firms which were not yet internationally competitive. The implications of this belief were that only those sectors which were perceived as internationally competitive should be open to foreign investment.

The issue of what should be the appropriate foreign investment policy response therefore attracted considerable controversy. According to the free market advocates, the way forward for industrial restructuring was to allow foreign firms to enter to compete with local firms thereby allowing the market to determine the future of the industrial structure. On the other hand those elements of the bureaucracy who favoured a more interventionist approach argued for the need to continue to protect various sectors of activity until those sectors had become competitive in accordance with the yardstick of international competition (Wade 1988) or until the necessary restructuring had been undertaken thereby ensuring that foreign firms would not gain domination of industry sectors.

The second issue in the debate was that of technology development. This issue became prominent towards the end of the 1980s when Korea's current account moved into surplus therefore leaving the interventionists with little room left to argue that Korea's manufacturing industries continued to need protection. The debate therefore turned to the continued protection of service industries and technology upgrading. As pointed out earlier, interventionists tend to see technology upgrading as lying at the heart of economic development and because of the late industrialisation phenomena also see a major role for the state in this process. Consequently the state should have policies in place such as joint venture rules, screening to allow only desired technology and tax incentives to attract the most technologically advanced foreign firms, to ensure that local firms do in fact benefit from the technology being introduced by foreign firms.

On the other hand the free market advocates argue against firm specific interventions to raise technological capability and more for what are termed functional interventions. These include measures such as promoting education and a suitable climate for research and development. This raises the absorptive capacity of society as a whole enabling local firms to adopt the technology necessary to compete with their foreign counterparts (Wade 1991; Lall 1994; Smith 1995). In a similar vein to their arguments set out above, the free market advocates suggest that specific measures such as tax incentives, investment screening and joint venture requirements will not necessarily produce technology transfer and at worst risk the possibility of the state targeting the wrong areas or officials succumbing to rent seeking pressures thereby resulting in misallocation of resources. For these reasons the best policy for technology acquisition is to leave it to market forces to allocate resources and to strengthen absorptive capacity through functional interventions. Since the debate regarding foreign investment's role in acquiring advanced technology only really began towards the end of the 1980s further consideration of it is deferred until chapter 6.

The structure of this chapter and the two following chapters is to first examine the economic and political environment that policy makers faced when framing policy followed by an analysis of foreign investment policy change and its outcomes and finally an assessment of the changes and outcomes in the light of the state's capacity in relation to this issue.

This chapter examines the 1979–85 period which coincides with the Chun Doo Hwan regime. The following two chapters also loosely coincide with Chun's successors. Each regime has established variations in its institutional features which has affected the capacity of the state in relation to foreign investment. Likewise each regime has confronted different external and internal circumstances within which policy had to be formulated and implemented. Differences of opinion over economic policy direction are most clear cut when analysed against the backdrop of the political and economic circumstances which confront policy makers at critical turning points. For these reasons it is useful to consider foreign investment in each time period.

The Rise of the Reformers

When General Chun Doo Hwan came to power in 1980, a significant movement was already underway to abandon the highly interventionist policies which had characterised the years of the HCI drive. A group of young American trained economists had convinced Park in the last months of his regime to begin to implement stabilisation measures to address the economic problems that had started to appear in the Korean economy (Rhee 1994: 93–103).

By 1980 these problems had become severe. The economy was plagued with a thirty per cent inflation rate caused by the rapid expansion of credit which had accompanied the policies to promote heavy and chemical industries and exacerbated by a 200 per cent increase in oil prices in 1979 (Choi B.S. 1991(a): 265). Serious over capacity existed in some of the heavy and chemical industries due to the allocation of duplicate projects to different companies (Rhee 1994: 92–3). The export performance which had played a large part in Korea's past growth was in jeopardy as a result of wage growth at twice that of productivity added to by the effects of inflation on the price of Korea's exports. This was all the more serious as export earnings were needed to service Korea's ballooning foreign debt which by 1980 had become the second largest in the developing world after Brazil (Woo 1991: 181). Finally confidence in the economy was badly shaken as a result of the political instability which had characterised the end of the Park regime with Chun Doo Hwan gradually consolidating his position after a coup on December 12 1979 until finally proclaiming himself president in September 1980. All of these problems were reflected in the economic growth rate which turned negative for the first time in nearly two decades.

To deal with these severe economic problems Chun sought advice from the foreign trained economists in the Economic Planning Board, who had earlier convinced Park of the need for a change in economic direction. The proposed measures very much accorded with neoclassical economic prescriptions. They included tighter monetary and fiscal policies to deal with inflationary problems in the short term and liberalisation of government controls over finance, imports and foreign investment to impose economic restructuring on Korea in line with its international competitive advantage for long term growth and stability (Rhee 1994: 94; Clifford 1994: 180). Chun's appointments to the key economic portfolios included people who were well known as economic reformers.

They included Kim Jae Ik as Chun's personal chief economic secretary and Shin Byong Hyun as the Deputy Prime Minister for the Economic Planning Board and later Kang Kyong Shik as Minister of Finance. Kim Jae Ik is widely recognised as the main architect of the reformist policies of the Chun era (Evans 1995; Rhee 1994: 87; Choi B.S. 1991(a): 167; Clifford 1994). His career in the EPB had provided him with all of the necessary credentials to be selected by Chun as his foremost economic policy adviser. As a reformer, Kim Jae Ik offered

Chun the prospect of a new start in economic policy and hence a measure of legitimacy if the reforms proved successful.

The liberalisation of foreign investment was very much on their agenda (Haggard 1988: 273; Haggard and Moon 1990: 220; Moon 1994: 147). The over reliance on loans as a source of finance for foreign capital had resulted in a significant drain on foreign exchange earnings due to increased servicing costs as a result of international interest rate rises. Increased levels of foreign investment were seen to be necessary to reduce the level of dependence on debt as well a means of continuing export growth without the debt servicing costs. The Far Eastern Economic Review drew attention to this at the time in the following terms:

> For the past several months, South Korea has been carrying out wide ranging economic reforms aimed at laying the foundation for continued growth with stability... The second broad area of reform is primarily aimed at inducing foreign capital. The government hopes that the combined effect of the reforms will be to stimulate a sluggish economy by financing investment more effectively and to stabilise the nations' balance of payments position by relying more on foreign capital inducement through foreign direct investment rather than foreign loans (*FEER* May 15, 1981: 57).

A switch to greater levels of foreign investment not only would provide a source of capital to replace loans but in line with neoclassical thinking was also seen as desirable at the time because of the favourable externalities resulting through technology transfer, increased international market linkages and competitive pressures to keep Korean industry efficient (Kim C.J. 1988: 192). Additionally, if foreign investment was to play a role in providing resources to areas of comparative advantage in the economy, then its liberalisation was a necessary accompaniment to the proposed trade liberalisation measures (*FEER* Dec 4 1981: 90). Without simultaneous liberalisation of both areas choices by foreigners regarding trade or investment might be guided more by market imperfections than market principles. There was also a need to liberalise foreign investment in line with trends in other developing countries which were beginning to see foreign investment as a more desirable alternative than foreign loans for financing economic development.

Of more pressing concern was the withdrawal of large numbers of firms in 1979 and 1980. These two years had seen the withdrawal of two of Korea's largest investors, Gulf Oil and Union Oil which had invested on a joint venture basis in two of Korea's four petroleum refineries (Koo 1982: 17). Gulf had been forced to withdraw because of legal problems it was encountering in the United States due to allegations that it had been engaged in bribery of the Park regime during the 1971 election campaign and Union Oil withdrew as a part of reassessment of its overall operations (Mardon 1990(a): 132–3). In addition large numbers of the smaller Japanese firms which had relocated to Korea in the early 1970s continued a withdrawal from Korea which had begun in 1976 (*FEER* July 9 1976: 44).

Policy Reforms and Outcomes

In accordance with the advice which he received from the free market advocates, Chun Doo Hwan proclaimed in his inauguration speech in 1980 that 'we will maintain the open system of international economic relations and will solidify our economic cooperation by boldly inducing foreign capital and technology' (Chun quoted in Kim C.J. 1988: 192). The first step taken by the reform group was to transfer the jurisdiction over foreign investment policy away from the Economic Planning Board to the Ministry of Finance with the proviso that the MOF was required to consult with other relevant ministries during the approval process (*FEER* Feb 19 1982: 42; Willis 1985: 1034). This indicated a shift away from the past approach of channelling foreign investment into selected sectors in accordance with government plans and priorities to one in which foreign investment was seen as simply another source of capital which could be utilised in the development process. The EPB's past association with planning together with the MOF's traditional jurisdiction over finance may well have led top policy makers to the belief that the MOF was the more appropriate agency to deal with the more market oriented approach proposed for foreign investment.

The transfer of jurisdiction to the MOF was followed by a slow process of revision of the Foreign Capital Inducement Law. This commenced in 1981 when the foreign investment division of the Ministry of Finance as the section responsible for foreign investment policy, began working on changes to the existing law. The major initiative of the new law, which eventually came into effect in 1984, was to change the previous policy regarding sectors open to investment. Prior to the new law, foreign investors had been largely confined to those sectors where foreign investments was said to be 'encouraged'. However even before the new law came into effect there had been some relaxation of the previous joint venture policy in a very limited range of industries. At the same time, an expansion had occurred in the number of industries in which foreign investment could proceed by way of joint venture rather than being totally excluded (*FEER* May 15 1981: 90). The new law formalised and extended these initiatives by declaring all sectors as being open to foreign investors unless they fell into either a restricted or prohibited category (*Business Korea* Aug 1984: 48).

There were a number of criteria pursuant to which the bureaucracy could designate an industry to be restricted. These included industries that were particularly supported by the state or infant industries considered for industrial policy reasons to need a certain period of protection (MOF 1993: 205). This demonstrated a continuation of the approach which sought to exclude foreign investment from certain sectors of the economy. It also demonstrated the ability of lower level bureaucrats to water down the free market approach advocated by top policy makers. The breadth of the restricted categories attracted complaints from foreign investors and to placate these concerns a further range of manufacturing industries were moved from the restricted category to the open category in 1985 (*Business Korea* July 1985: 72–5).

A system of automatic approval was also introduced by the 1984 law. However, the reluctance of working level officials to relinquish control over the process was evident from the narrow range of investments to which the automatic approval system was made applicable. Automatic approval was only possible if the foreign equity in the project was less than 50 per cent, the investment amount was less than US $1 million, no claim for tax reduction was made and the investment did not fall into a restricted category (*Business Korea* Aug 1984: 48). This left a rather limited category of investments which did not need to undergo the rigorous examination system of the Ministry of Finance and other ministries who had an interest in the area of the investment. The result was that there were significant opportunities available for the other ministries to block foreign investments if it was felt that they would cause harm to existing Korean firms in those industries.

The other major changes to the law included a provision that allowed up to 100 per cent ownership. In 1982 Chun foreshadowed this change in policy when he said:

> In the past when foreign companies wanted to invest in Korea there was too much red tape involved because the government wanted to regulate and control them. My policy is to eliminate this red tape as much as possible and to drastically simplify administrative procedures. I have made instructions to this effect and studies are being made to improve the investment climate. In the past foreigners weren't allowed a share over 50 per cent but I am going to allow foreign investors to go up to 100 per cent (Selected Speeches of Chun Doo Hwan, Vol. 1 1982: 222).

Changes were also made to the system of tax incentives. Prior to the new law there had been some concern that foreign firms in some areas

were eligible for tax reduction when Korean firms were not (*FEER* May 7
1976: 89). The changes meant incentives for foreign firms were reduced
so that tax incentives were only available if the investment made a
significant contribution to the international balance of payments, if it was
accompanied by advanced technology or a very large amount of capital
or if it was to be located in a free export zone (*Business Korea* Aug 1984:
48). The time period for which tax exemption was granted remained
similar to the previous policy. The major change was that the number of
eligible firms was significantly reduced.

While the top policy makers aimed to significantly liberalise policy
with the introduction of a completely new law, it can be seen from the
above analysis that many of the changes were only incremental. The
foreign investor community had been critical of the new government's
approach since the early 1980s and the new law did little to ease their
concerns.

The foreign investor community lamented the initial change of
jurisdiction over foreign investment from the Economic Planning Board
to the Ministry of Finance. They argued that although the EPB had been
seen as restrictive, it at least had a positive attitude to foreign investment.
The major complaints centred on the consultation procedures which had
to be conducted with other ministries and which provided those ministries
with the opportunity to block foreign investment proposals (Willis 1985:
1043). The Far Eastern Economic Review summarised the situation in the
following terms:

> There are complaints that some of the other ministries are staffed by officials
> unfriendly to the idea of foreign investment.... and that their ties to the local
> business community dominate their decisions. The result is that the
> principles and guidelines issued by the Blue House and the Finance Ministry,
> which generally favour the foreign investor, are mired in the case by case
> dealings of the other ministries (*FEER* Feb 19, 1982: 42).

Similar views to these were again expressed by foreign investors at a
seminar organised by the Korea Development Institute in September
1983 (*Economist* Sep 17, 1983: 80). To give some weight to their
criticisms of the new system, foreign investors pointed to the increasing
numbers of rejections being received by foreign investors even in areas
where there was a demonstrable benefit to the Korean economy from the
proposed project (*IBW* December 6 1982: 38–9).

The cause of these difficulties lay not so much in the consultation
procedures which had existed even during the period of the EPB's reign,
but in the inability of the Ministry of Finance to override the objections
of the other ministries. The structurally powerful position of the EPB had

meant that it could override other ministries. The MOF on the other hand had no such standing in the bureaucracy. There were also some suggestions that some officials in the Ministry of Finance were as protectionist as the other ministries and opposed to foreign investment (Willis 1985: 1047).

The complaints did not subside with the introduction of the new law in 1984. A British Chamber of Commerce spokesman was quoted as commenting that it did little to ease the problem of the different views that existed within the bureaucracy concerning the desirability of foreign investment (*Business Korea* Aug 1984: 49). Lower level officials were seen as creating bottlenecks by interpreting regulations narrowly and citing unpublished internal guidelines as the reasons for rejecting investment (*Business Korea* July 1985: 76; *FEER* Apr 4 1985: 66). The protectionist attitude of some parts of the bureaucracy was reported to have even been noted by the president of the Korea Development Institute (KDI), Kim Ki Hwan who allegedly told a US Chamber of Commerce gathering that government attempts at reform were being thwarted by lower level officials (*Business Korea* August 1985: 23). By 1987 foreign investors were still complaining that although they knew people at the top wanted liberalisation the message was becoming lost somewhere on the way down and that only a third of foreign investment was proceeding by way of wholly owned investment because joint ventures were still frowned upon by government officials (*Business Korea* October 1987: 27).

There is a sufficiency of evidence to show that protection of Korean industry was a major motivating factor for the approach of working level bureaucrats. For example, as noted earlier, the grounds for rejecting many foreign investment applications were that they would damage local business (*FEER* Feb 19 1982: 42). Further, when the new foreign capital inducement law came into force industries could be classified as restricted if they were in need of continuing protection and government support. Even when the US was able to pressure Korea into opening a further 102 sectors to foreign investment in 1985, some sectors such as advertising and cosmetics which the US had specifically requested be opened remained closed due to the bureaucracy considering that to open those industries would cause undue harm to local producers (*Business Korea* Nov 1985: 54). Finally, the transfer of jurisdiction over foreign investment meant that it was easier to protect local firms if any relevant ministry thought it desirable to do so (*FEER* Apr 4 1985: 66).

The unsuccessful attempts by the free market advocates to remove restrictions on foreign investment were matched by a lack of success in allowing the free market to determine its allocation. The amounts of investment that were attracted were also a disappointment to those who believed that greater amounts of foreign investment would lead to benefits through its provision of capital and associated spinoffs of technology and competition for local industries.

Foreign investment and its distribution by industry for the 1979 to 1986 period is set out in Table 4.1.

A feature of foreign investment flows during the period was the continuation of its industrial distribution among the same sectors that had dominated it in the 1973–79 period. This points to consistency with the priorities of the previous regime rather than the bold new approach advocated by Chun. Of the total amount of manufacturing investment, chemical industries and the electronics industry accounted for over 50 per cent.

There was little investment in the service industries other than in the finance sector. This followed some liberalisation of the Korean financial system in the early 1980s which denationalised the commercial banks and allowed the establishment of non bank financial intermediaries. Foreign firms sought to take advantage of this liberalisation and although investment in this area remained restricted some foreign banks were able to pressure the Korean government to allow the establishment of branches mainly to service their own customers in Korea. The other areas which showed continued investment from the previous period included the hotel industry and some further investment in the construction industry.

Objective measures of the reform efforts also give credence to the complaints by foreign investors that the reform efforts had achieved little. One of the aims of the free market advocates was to increase foreign investment. In fact the fifth five year plan proposed a $2.5 billion dollar increase (*FEER* May 14, 1982: 67). Only $1.1 billion arrived. The attempt to diversify sources of foreign capital away from foreign loans and towards foreign investment also had little success. The percentage of foreign investment in foreign capital inflow remained relatively low at only 7–10 per cent for most of the 1979–86 time period as Table 4.2 shows.

Further, while there was some new investment from well known computer companies such as IBM and Hewlett Packard and a number of major electronics firms including Tandy, Honeywell and AT&T, there is evidence that much of the investment during the period was by way of additional capital introduced by firms which were already established in Korea. In 1982, for example, two thirds of the US investment was to provide additional working capital for existing firms (*FEER* May 14 1982: 67). Much of the investment in the transport equipment industry was by way of additional investment by General Motors to expand its joint venture with Daewoo in car production.

Table 4.1: Foreign Direct Investment by Industry (1979–85)
(US million dollars)

Industry	1979	1980	1981	1982	1983	1984	1985	1979–85 $	%
Agriculture Livestock, Fishery	1	–	1	1	–	1	–	4	0.3
Mining	–	–	–	–	–	–	1	1	0.1
Manufacturing	111	97	115	112	72	29	168	803	69.3
Fibre/Garment	–	–	1	3	2	2	–	8	0.7
Timber and Paper	–	1	3	7	1	1	5	18	1.6
Food	11	–	12	6	8	12	5	54	4.7
Chemical	41	47	49	34	6	5	20	202	17.5
Medicines	2	–	5	7	9	18	8	50	4.3
Fertilisers	2	–	–	–	1	–	–	3	0.3
Petroleum	4	8	–	–	1	5	–	19	1.6
Ceramic	2	1	2	–	–	1	–	6	0.5
Metals	8	5	14	2	1	5	4	38	3.3
Machinery	21	7	7	2	2	6	6	51	4.4
Electric/Electronic	15	18	22	27	25	63	38	208	18.0
Transport Equip	3	8	1	22	16	8	79	137	11.8
Other manufactures	1	1	–	2	–	2	3	9	0.8
Services	83	34	36	16	50	64	66	349	33.0
Finance and Insurance	49	13	7	10	27	14	20	140	12.3
Construction	–	–	9	–	1	10	20	40	3.5
Transport/Storage	3	13	2	1	1	1	1	22	1.9
Hotels	21	3	6	3	20	37	9	99	8.6
Wholesale and Retail	–	–	–	–	–	–	15	15	1.3
Total	195	131	152	128	122	193	236	1157	100.0

Source: Ministry of Finance 1993: 238, Table 5–27

The objective of increasing the ability of foreign firms to invest by way of wholly owned projects was also unsuccessful. Despite Chun Doo Hwan having signalled an intention that this would be permitted and foreign investors' assertions that they would be reluctant to invest unless it was, government officials were reportedly unwilling to approve wholly owned foreign investment proposals (*Business Korea* July 1985: 76–7). During the 1973–78 period wholly owned investment averaged 5.3 per cent in terms of the number of cases and 30.4 per cent by way of amount. During the 1979–85 period, wholly owned investment increased to only 9 per cent by way of the number of cases and fell to 22 per cent of the total in terms of investment amount (MOF 1993 Table 4–24: 180 and Table 5–28: 240).

Table 4.2: Shifts in Loans and Foreign Investments in Korea (US million dollars; %)

Years	Total	Loan		Foreign Investment	
		Public	Private	Amount	Per cent
1983	2568	1493	974	101	(3.9)
1984	2454	1424	859	171	(7.0)
1985	2224	1024	964	236	(10.6)
1986	2976	880	1619	477	(16.0)
1987	3293	1109	1558	626	(19.0)
1988	2773	891	988	894	(32.4)
1989	2147	475	860	812	(37.8)
1990	1343	418	30	895	(66.6)
1991	1603	429	–	1174	(73.2)
1992	1439	486	150	803	(56.0)

Source: Ministry of Finance, Fiscal and Financial Statistics, 1993.

Continued government involvement in most investment approvals is evident from the extent to which foreign investors used the automatic approval system. Between 1984 when a limited automatic approval system was introduced and 1987, only 20 per cent of investment fell into the automatic approval category (Koo and Bark 1988: 32) leaving it open in 80 per cent of cases for the bureaucracy to impose conditions on foreign investors should this be desired. The gap between bureaucratic practice and top policy makers' ideals in this area is reflected in Chun's aims for the automatic approval system expressed in an interview in 1982:

> Furthermore in so far as applications for investment are concerned, part of our policy, as incorporated in the fifth five year plan that begins next year is to adopt what is called a negative list approach, whereby all proper foreign investment applications will be automatically approved except in a few restricted areas that will be specified in advance (Selected Speeches of Chun Doo Hwan, Vol. 5: 257).

The lack of success of reform efforts and the poor performance of foreign investment can be attributed to a considerable degree to the lack of acceptance of the objectives of the free market reformers by lower level bureaucrats. However, the poor performance was also due to other factors which were not directly related to the reform program. In 1982, Korea's largest single investor, the Dow Chemical company, with investments comprising in excess of 10 per cent of Korea's total foreign investment stocks was in dispute with a joint venture partner in one if its projects. Dow had wanted to buy out its joint venture partner but they had refused to sell. The issue had not been confined to inter-company wrangling but had also attracted political intervention. The head of Dow's US branch, Robert Lundeen, had raised the issue in discussions with economic ministers and had even been given an audience with Chun Doo Hwan indicating the concern that reformers felt about the impact of this dispute on their aim of encouraging more foreign investment (*FEER* June 11 1982: 120–1). The bitterness of the dispute eventually led to Dow withdrawing all of its investment from Korea. Unfavourable coverage of Korea's foreign investment environment followed in the foreign press making the reformers' efforts at liberalisation and attracting foreign investment that much more difficult (*FEER* Oct 22 1982: 105).

The free market advocates also suffered a setback in 1983 when Kim Jae Ik, the president's chief economic secretary and several other government ministers were killed in a terrorist attack in Rangoon. It has already been noted that Kim Jae Ik was the driving force behind the reform effort. At a time when the group of reformers were still small in number the loss of a person of this stature significantly lessened the momentum.

By 1985, the initial burst of reforms appeared to have run its course. Opposition to the general thrust of the liberalisation strategy of the government began to move beyond the bureaucracy with the economy again encountering another slowdown and the approach of elections for the National Assembly. Korea's international economic relations including foreign investment had been a major issue in the campaign with senior policy makers coming under attack from all sides for having proceeded too fast with liberalisation. The American trained economists who had been directing government economic policy during the Chun regime were singled out for particular criticism by the press and by some government ministers (*Business Korea* August 1985: 22–33). The Head of the Korea Development Institute, Kim Ki Hwan, was a particular target. Not only had he been educated in the US even teaching at the University of California, Berkeley, but he was also the head of the International Economic Policy Council which had been established in 1983 to further Korea's internationalisation. Kim was branded a 'US sympathiser' who was using the International Economic Policy Council to pursue liberalisation in the interests of the US rather than in the interests of Korea. In 1986, the Council was abolished (Choi 1991(a)).

Chun Doo Hwan and State Capacity

Bureaucratic capacity during the Park era had hinged upon the wide acceptance of a developmental ideology which placed a strong emphasis on the role of the state in guiding and directing economic activity even to the level of the individual firm (Jones and Sakong 1980). While there had always been some dissent within the bureaucracy concerning the role of the state in economic development, its internal features effectively prevented any ideological cleavages from having an impact on the policy making process during the Park era (Haggard 1988: 262). The manner in which Park was able to establish a series of new institutions and bureaucratic alliances to ensure implementation of his policies for heavy industry led industrialisation provides solid evidence for this. In the Chun era an ideological division concerning economic policy and the lack of institutional mechanisms for the resolution of this difference of opinion resulted in reduced bureaucratic capacity for policy reform.

Chun's initial concern was the need to attempt to secure some form of legitimacy for his regime. His accession to power through a military coup combined with the repressive measures which had been applied against the dissidents at Kwangju left his regime with little popular appeal (Lee M.W. 1990: 7). In order to secure some public support he was urged by the younger generals who had supported his coup to reorient the growth first policies of the Park era towards policies which favoured distribution and welfare (Haggard and Moon 1990: 219). On the other hand, he was urged by the reformers in his administration to move quickly towards a market oriented economy as the best means for restoring rapid economic growth and hence legitimacy.

Chun accepted the argument of his economic advisers to move from the past strategy of state led development to one in which the free market would be the primary determinant of economic development (Kim E.M. 1988: 116; Kim and Lim 1994: 137; MacIntyre 1990:14; Lee and Lee 1992: 15; Kim B.W. 1991: 137). It was this break in economic development strategy which signalled the end of the dominance of the previously prevailing developmental ideology and a continuing debate within the state concerning its proper role in the economy. It has been this debate which has been at the root of the difficulties in economic policy making which have occurred since that time. This has produced a sense of confusion within the state concerning the economic orientation that the state should take (Kim E.M. 1993: 243), a situation which Rhee has characterised as being 'lost between state and market' (Rhee 1994: 236).

The group of young American trained economists who advised first Park and then Chun to move towards a market oriented economy have been described as having acquired their views from their training in the principles of laissez faire economics in doctoral programs in the United States (Amsden 1994(a): 94–7; Haggard and Moon 1990: 218; Johnson 1994: 74–5; Clifford 1994: 177; *FEER* May 14 1982: 72). Once ensconced in positions of influence they naturally sought to apply those principles to the Korean economy of the 1980s which in any event left itself open to an alternative approach due to the economic problems described earlier.

This group met with significant opposition in the bureaucracy as has been noted. Only the elite had had the opportunity for foreign training and the ordinary bureaucrat continued to be influenced by a tradition which had emphasised the prominence of the state rather than the market in influencing economic activity. The withdrawal of the state from a strongly interventionist role in economic activity would have also resulted in less power for the bureaucracy. It is partly for this reason that past patterns of intervention were extremely difficult to change (Kuznets 1994; 129: 236; Smith 1995; Doner 1992: 400; Choi and Lee 1995) and partly because of the effectiveness of past policies towards foreign investment from the interventionists' point of view.

Features of Chun's leadership style reinforced the difficulties caused by the ideological divide. Chun was not able to resolve the internal differences of opinion because he had neither sufficient experience in economic management nor was he inclined towards the attention to the details of economic policy that characterised Park's leadership style. This was reinforced by his relative lack of knowledge in the economic policy area as well as the greater complexity that the economy had acquired after two decades of economic growth. He preferred to set the broad goals of economic policy leaving the details to the relevant ministers and bureaucrats (Chung C.K. 1989; Moon and Prasad 1994: 365). An added impetus to Chun's decision to delegate economic affairs to experts lay in the severe economic problems which the economy confronted at the commencement of his term of office.

The old military like command structure and appeal to traditional cultural values of deference for the leader which had served to reinforce cohesiveness in the bureaucracy in the Park era also declined under Chun because of a certain lack of respect which lower level bureaucrats held for his regime. Chun had shown a willingness to deal harshly with the bureaucracy. Upon coming to power he had purged several thousand bureaucrats who came from all levels of the civil service (Haggard and Moon 1990: 221). This move together with the increasing rate at which civil servants were falling behind in living standards meant that morale was at a low level increasing the tendency of bureaucrats to protect their own positions wherever possible and at the same time to do no more than was necessary to remain employed (Jun 1985). In this environment the prospects for enthusiasm for policy change and diligent implementation of it were significantly reduced (Kim Y.H. 1994: 53).

In addition, a number of financial scandals occurred involving Chun's relatives. This badly tarnished Chun's credibility in economic policy in the eyes of the bureaucracy making his regime's pledge to build a just society sound increasingly hollow (Yoon Y.O. 1990: 75). Chung C.K. (1986) and Kim E.M. (1993: 239) also note that at times policy initiatives were conflicting leaving bureaucrats in a difficult position regarding implementation. All of these factors reinforced the reluctance of bureaucrats to implement any liberalisation measures which would further detract from their power base.

Kim Y.H. (1994: 52–3) also attributes the lack of success of the free market advocates to the failure of the Chun regime to change the institutional structure of the state. The continuing dominance of the executive branch under the constitutional arrangements adopted by the Chun regime in 1980 meant that there was little possibility for other formal state institutions, such as the National Assembly, playing a role in resolving internal conflicts over policy direction. While legitimacy concerns resulted in the new constitution formally providing the national assembly with some power over presidential actions including a revival of the power for it to investigate the bureaucracy (Hinton 1983: 62–3; Yoon Y.O. 1991: 144), the steps taken by the Chun regime to ensure domination of the national assembly by his own party resulted in little erosion of executive dominance. These included a ban on political activities of leading opponents to the previous Park regime including Kim Young Sam and Kim Dae Jung and active repression of unofficial opposition through the use of state force and press censorship. The continuation of an electoral system based upon two member districts and proportional representation aimed to ensure that Chun's Democratic Justice Party would dominate the national assembly precluding the effective expression of societal opposition to the regime's policies through this forum.

The effectiveness of foreign investment policy in the Park era had depended upon the internal cohesiveness of the bureaucracy. The difference of opinion that arose between top policy makers and working level bureaucrats concerning foreign investment policy may have been able to be resolved had jurisdiction over it remained with the EPB. In the Chun era, the EPB came to assume even more power than it had held under Park because of Chun's propensity to delegate (Choi B.S. 1991(a)). In this respect the decision to transfer the authority over foreign investment from the EPB to the Ministry of Finance had significant implications. In the past, such disputes were able to be resolved by the EPB because it had jurisdiction over foreign investment policy and because of its power within the bureaucracy. The Ministry of Finance lacked sufficient legal or moral authority to force any particular view on other ministries. Thus policy change was an affair of compromise resulting in far less change than hoped for by those at the top.

While the Council of Economic Minsters was established as a formal body to resolve disputes between ministries, disputes in the realm of foreign investment policy lay not only in major changes in policy but also in the minutiae of the regulations and their implementation. Matters of policy were able to be compromised at the departmental and Ministerial level leading to some change in the law although not to the degree that the free market advocates would have wanted. The implementation of policy on the other hand was left to lower level officials across a range of departments with no effective mechanisms available to reconcile conflicting views.

Chun's propensity to leave the details of economic policy making to the technocrats in the EPB and the senior economic secretaires also meant that he was not able to arbitrate as effectively as Park in solving serious economic policy disputes at the senior level. Similarly the high turnover of ministers during his regime (Chung C.K. 1989) meant that their role in acting as arbitrators between conflicting views in the bureaucracy was also limited. Chun's break with past practice by appointing outside experts rather than experts from the bureaucracy to ministerial positions and senior positions on his personal economic staff meant that the potential for disagreement between those outside experts and the bureaucracy was heightened (Chung C.K. 1989).

Therefore while it was possible for top policy makers to proclaim a more liberalised policy, it was at the lower levels of the bureaucracy where policy details were formulated and implementation occurred that reform objectives became stalled.

During the Chun era the state remained in a powerful position in relation to social forces. While the bureaucracy utilised the informal networks which had been established over many years to consult with the business community regarding foreign investment policy and its implementation (USITC 1989: D4), the structural power of the bureaucracy and the inability for any group to effectively challenge it led to it being left to determine what lay in the best interests of Korea as far as foreign investment was concerned. As will be seen societal interests commenced to have an impact in the democratised environment of the post 1987 period.

Conclusion

The effectiveness of the state's intervention in foreign investment matters which had characterised the Park era began to unravel from 1980 when a split developed within the bureaucracy concerning the future economic policy direction of the Korean state. Despite the appointment of persons favouring significant reform to senior policy making positions within the Korean state, only limited results were achieved in terms of actual policy changes and policy outcomes.

Foreign investment flows failed to constitute a more significant source of external capital during the period and the industries into which it flowed showed a continuation of past patterns. Foreign investors were highly critical of the conflicting signals being given to them by top policy makers and working level bureaucrats particularly when they had been accustomed to a highly cohesive and competent bureaucratic approach.

The failure of the reform effort during the period can be attributed to a reluctance of many parts of the bureaucracy to abandon the interventionist policies of the past. The liberalisation measures proposed by the reformers were not only seen as causing potential damage to their constituents but were also a threat to their ability to continue to manage economic activity in what they considered to be Korea's best interests. The institutional features of the state in the Chun era continued the structural power of the bureaucracy but failed to provide adequate mechanisms for the resolution of internal disputes. The features of the institutional arrangements had in the past resulted in the president and key advisers playing such a role. It has been noted already that in the Park era bureaucratic capacity hinged upon the internal structuring of the bureaucracy, the wide acceptance of a developmental ideology and Park's leadership style. However Chun Doo Hwan's personal leadership style and legitimacy constraints all militated against effective leadership on economic issues at the presidential level during his term of office. When combined with the shift away from universal acceptance of the old ideology of developmentalsim and the changed constitutional arrangements, it is not surprising that foreign investment policy failed to achieve the objective of top policy makers.

The exclusionist and repressive policies which the Chun regime continued to pursue in relation to society at large meant that there was little societal input into policy matters other than through the national assembly. The assembly itself was constrained due to the constitutional arrangements and Chun's domination of the majority party. Some pressure arose only as the 1985 elections approached when government party members fearing the effects of change on their constituents argued for preservation of the status quo rather than reform.

5 Roh Tae Woo and the Slow Down of Foreign Investment Policy Reform

Introduction

The state's capacity for sound policy formulation and implementation has the effect of raising living standards to the degree that people begin to demand political development as well as economic development (Kim E.M. 1993: 232). In order to maintain legitimacy the state must eventually respond and because of this it becomes difficult to maintain its insulation in policy making (Rueschemeyer and Evans 1985: 49). In these circumstances, the continuation of policies which rely for their effectiveness on the exclusion of the interests of societal actors becomes impossible to sustain (Johnson 1989: 6; 1994: 76).

A diminution in the state's insulation from societal actors can also lead to reduced bureaucratic capacity (Evans, Rueschemeyer and Skocpol 1985: 354) because the penetration of the state by societal groups may widen any internal cleavages which exist. During the Chun era, the erosion of the bureaucratic capacity of the state had been largely responsible for the difficulties in foreign investment policy change. On this particular issue the state had been able to keep itself relatively insulated from societal pressures. The state bureaucracy formulated and implemented policy based upon its opinion of what was in the best interests of its constituents rather than on the basis of constituent's demands. As has been seen, there were conflicting opinions concerning the best policy options to pursue these interests.

In the Roh era the bureaucratic capacity of the state continued to be plagued by the ideological division between the free market advocates and the interventionists. This was reinforced by structural changes that Roh made to the institutions of the state which further reduced the effectiveness of mechanisms for resolving conflicts between top policy makers and lower level bureaucrats. Foreign investment policy change was made even more difficult because the institutions of the state were unable to resolve the conflicting societal pressures that emerged regarding deregulation generally. On the one hand, interests representing big business favoured deregulation but this faced popular opposition expressed by the labour movement, the national assembly and the press. The inability to resolve competing societal concerns regarding deregulation generally, reinforced the internal divisions concerning foreign investment deregulation in particular.

This chapter first sets out the environment within which policy choices had to be made. It traces the roots of societal pressure for policy change to the repressive policies of the Chun era and highlights the impact of these domestic political changes and international events on the economic environment confronting policy makers. It then examines foreign investment policy change during the Roh era. It concludes that little policy change occurred and that the outcomes reflect this. Finally, the chapter returns to the issue of the state's reduced capacity for reform as an explanation for these outcomes. It emphasises the reduced ability of the state to insulate itself from competing societal demands and the effect that this had in exacerbating the internal division between top policy makers and working level bureaucrats.

The Influence of the Domestic and International Environment in the Roh Era

The domestic and international political and economic environment confronting policy makers underwent a major shift in 1986–87. As noted previously it is necessary to consider foreign investment policies against the backdrop of changes in this environment. Of most significance was the changed domestic political situation from 1987. In mid 1987, Chun Doo Hwan had effectively been swept from power by a people's revolution which had been led by those political leaders who since the beginning of his regime had been excluded from holding formal political positions. It had attracted wide support from student groups, church leaders, workers and finally the middle classes in Seoul.

The grievances which the population had against the Chun regime emanated from Chun's undemocratic accession to power and the bloody suppression of an uprising in Kwangju in 1980. This set the tone of the regime which throughout its term did not hesitate to use the coercive powers of the state against any form of opposition from political leaders, labour unions, intellectuals or students (Shaw 1991; Lee M.W. 1990: 111–14). As Moon and Kim (forthcoming: 16) note, by the end of his regime there were few sections of the population that had not been isolated by his administration. The beginnings of this isolation of societal groups can be traced to the closing years of the Park regime.

The pattern of industrial growth during the 1970s had led to a change in work force composition away from light industries and towards the heavy industrial sector. Accompanying this change were increased levels of unionisation due to the changed nature of workplaces and increased demands for political participation. (Koo 1992: 678; Lie 1991: 507). The formation of a peoples (minjung) movement toward the end of the 1970s by labour, church and student groups hastened the end of the Park regime through the political instability which occurred after this loose coalition of forces narrowly lost the 1978 national assembly elections. The reaction of the incoming Chun regime was to instigate a purge of the leadership of the FKTU which had been demanding continuing wage rises in line with productivity increases (Deyo 1989(a): 138; Haggard and Moon 1990: 224) and to replace the heads of all 11 national unions with persons selected by the regime (Launius 1984: 11). Through an amendment of the labour laws, industry wide collective bargaining was discontinued and was replaced by a system of enterprise based unionism (Deyo Haggard and Koo 1987: 47; Kim and Lim 1994: 13). Labour disputes between company and employees were to be dealt with by the state with third parties being banned from intervening (Haggard and Moon 1990: 224; Choi J.J. 1989). The coercive agencies of the state continued to be used to prevent the escalation of industrial actions at the workplace (Launius 1984: 6).

As well as containing the political activity of workers, the Chun regime also actively sought to restrain wage growth and failed to pay attention to demands for improvements in working conditions (Deyo 1987). In the early 1980s, Koreans worked longer hours than anywhere else in the industrialising world and had the worst record of industrial accidents (Lie 1990: 505) and yet average weekly earnings were shown to be below the poverty line (Launius 1984: 8; Lee M.W. 1990: 42). The overtly oppressive state arrested and detained more persons for political activities than during the entire Park period (Moon and Kim forthcoming: 11).

The final event which brought the middle classes onto the streets in June of 1987 was the death by torture of a young student activist from Seoul National University (Lee M.W. 1990: 36). Buoyed by the recent success of a people's power revolution which had replaced the Marcos dictatorship in the Philippines as well as the knowledge that Chun was constrained in the overt use of force against demonstrators because of the international spotlight placed on Korea with the approaching Olympic games, the leaders of the demonstration sought and obtained a range of democratic reforms encapsulated in the statement proclaimed by Roh Tae Woo on 29 June 1987 (Lee M.W. 1990: 39).

The economic environment which confronted the incoming Roh administration could scarcely have been more different to that which confronted his predecessor. The three lows as they have been called (Woo 1991; Koo and Kim 1992: 143; Nam S.W. 1991) had resulted in Korea achieving a significant favourable balance in its current account in 1986 (Nam S.W. 1991: 12). Low international oil prices, the low exchange rate of the Won compared to the Japanese yen and low international interest rates had made Korean exports more competitive in international markets. The price competitiveness had also been assisted by Chun's repressive labour policies which had significantly held down wages growth (Launius 1984: 9; Lie 1990: 505).

Towards the end of 1989, the Korean economy again showed signs of problems. After the repressive labour policies of the Chun years, the declaration of 29 June 1987 had signalled a change in the state's attitude to industrial action and unleashed the pent up tide of labour demands (Lee M.W. 1990: 42; Kim E.M. 1993: 235). The number of strikes increased from around 276 cases in 1986 to over 3500 in 1987 (Kim E.M. 1993: 235). The number of work days lost due to strikes rose from 72,025 in 1986 to nearly 7 million in 1987 and remained at levels of 5 and 6 million for 1989 and 1990 respectively (Moon and Kim forthcoming: 23, Table 2). There was also an explosion in the growth of the number of unions which included the formation of several new national industry wide unions without the sanction of the state (Moon and Kim forthcoming: 22).

In addition, and despite government attempts to prevent it, the second half of the 1980s had seen the major conglomerates investing in speculative ventures in real estate and the stock market rather than in areas which would directly increase output (*Business Korea* Nov 1989: 22–3; Lee and Lee 1992: 15; Rhee 1994: 237). The result was a slow down in the rate of economic growth. Following a merger in January 1990 between two of the opposition parties and Roh's Democratic Justice Party to form the Democratic Liberal Party, government party members placed further pressure upon the administration to turn the economy around (*Business Korea* March 1990: 44–5).

As in the past it was the free market advocates occupying key economic posts who were held accountable for the economic downturn. Roh dismissed his Deputy Prime Minister for the Economic Planning Board, his chief economic secretary and several other economic ministers replacing them with those who could be relied upon to support a major shift in economic policy which aimed at rekindling economic growth (*Business Korea* April 1990: 23–4; Rhee 1994: 236–7; *FEER* May 1990: 44–5; Clifford 1994: 308). A meeting of the cabinet on April 4 1990 endorsed a range of growth first policies which would provide increased assistance to industry to expand investment and thereby increase exports (*Business Korea* May 1990: 18). Renewed repression of union activity and the labour movement generally occurred in a bid to hold down increases in labour costs (*FEER* June 28 1990: 37–8; Kim and Lim 1994: 24). Policies which had been proposed to restrain the speculative investments by the chaebols were shelved. At the same time there was an attempt to reduce the trade deficit by an unofficial policy of blocking imports with non tariff barriers (Clifford 1994: 308).

The entire period of Roh Tae Woo's rule was beset by domestic political problems which had flow on effects for Korea's economy and economic policy making. As will be seen this environment made it difficult to devise and implement foreign investment policy change in line with the objectives of top policy makers in the regime.

Foreign Investment Policy Change and Outcomes

During the Roh era there was little progress towards a more market oriented foreign investment policy. The incremental nature of changes in policy in the area of the approvals system, sectoral opening and reduction of tax incentives highlights this.

The Ministry of Finance continued to exercise rights of approval over most categories of foreign investment throughout the period. Although the automatic approval system introduced in 1984 had been extended in 1988 and again in 1991 (MOF 1993: 260–4), it only applied to investments in which foreign investors held a minority interest, in areas that were not on the restricted list and for which foreign investors were not eligible for tax incentives. As will be shown below investors were most interested in the service sector which for the most part remained on the restricted list. Consequently the government's policy change had minimal effect in reducing the bureaucratic obstacles for most categories of intending investors.

The opening of sectors to foreign investors had begun in the early 1980s as shown in the previous chapter. During the Roh era only incremental change occurred in this area. In 1987 a further 26 manufacturing sectors were opened to foreign investment. While this resulted in an increase in the liberalisation ratio in the manufacturing sectors from around 95 per cent to some 97 per cent, it still did not address the issue of service industries. It was becoming increasingly apparent that the main interest for foreign investors was in this sector. A number of surveys had shown that the domestic market, which includes service industries, was the major target for firms thinking of investing in Korea (Koo and Bark 1988: 25; *Financial Times* May 16 1990). The rapid increase in costs due to the wage rises over the 1987–89 period had eroded Korea's international competitiveness. This meant that the interest of foreign investors in manufacturing oriented investment decreased. If Korea was to attract further investment in manufacturing, investors needed to have an ability to sell on the domestic market and establish supporting service industries. Yet, as Soo Gil Young points out, there was extreme reluctance to open the domestic market to foreign investors. He accurately predicted that this would be a major difficulty in US-Korea relations in the years to come (Young S.G. 1988: 60). During the 1986–90 period only a few service industries were opened and these resulted from specific US requests. However specific conditions were also often attached.

For example, while pharmaceutical wholesaling, cosmetics wholesaling, advertising and travel agencies were opened to 100 per cent foreign ownership retailing in these areas was still restricted. Data communications, foreign securities firms and sea freight forwarding had a 50 per cent foreign ownership limit applied. Wholesaling of alcoholic beverages and insurance brokerage was allowed but both of these were subject to exclusive dealership arrangements (*East Asian Executive Reports* Jan 1990; March 1991).

The improved position in the balance of payments from 1986 provided less room for interventionists to argue that foreign investment should make a specific contribution to exports. This allowed the free market advocates who occupied top policy making positions at the time to ease export conditions which had frequently been imposed on foreign investors in the manufacturing sector. In 1987, restrictions relating to exports were relaxed to allow electronics producers to sell on the domestic market (MOF 1993: 264–8) and general requirements which had been imposed on many investors requiring them to export a percentage of their production were gradually removed from the end of 1989 (*East Asian Executive Reports* Jan 1990).

The reason for agreement being reached on this issue was not only the improved balance of payments position of the economy generally but also the improved position of foreign invested firms in particular. A study by the Ministry of Finance (1993: 435) for the 1980–90 period showed that it was only in 1987 that exports by foreign firms exceeded their imports for the first time. The removal of export conditions on foreign invested firms appears to have been a concession to the free market advocates by interventionist interests. However, this concession was only made because foreign firms were seen to be making a positive contribution to the economy and could now be released from conditions which had previously ensured that this would be the case.

Changes in the area of tax incentives also showed some concessions to the arguments of the free market advocates. In 1988 tax incentives were finally abolished for export oriented industries coinciding with Korea's favourable balance of trade figures. They became limited to those industries which would' bring in high technology (*Business Korea* July 1988). In 1991, the period for which tax exemption was granted was reduced from the previous five years to three years and the concession on the import of machinery and parts was reduced to 50 per cent from the previous full exemption (MOF 1993: 264; *KED* Feb 29 1992). While this appeared to be a concession to the reformers, the reason given at the time was to bring tax concessions between foreign firms and local firms into alignment rather than because of acceptance of the idea that tax incentives of themselves were not effective (*KED* Jan 7 1991).

These outcomes reflect only moderate success by the free market oriented top policy makers who dominated the economic ministries in the 1988–90 period. As noted, from 1990, Korea reversed economic policy direction towards a more interventionist and protectionist stance thereby reducing the possibility for further radical reforms. The only major achievement after this time was a commitment to introduce a notification system for foreign investments as a result of US complaints concerning the bureaucratic obstacles caused by the approval system. As will be seen in the following chapter this move was the thin edge of the wedge for those elements within the bureaucracy who continued to favour a highly interventionist approach.

The vacillation of the Roh government between a more market oriented policy and its reverse course from 1990 resulted in confusion in the foreign investor community concerning the intentions of the state. A survey by the Ministry of Trade and Industry in 1992 found that 'complicated rules' was perceived by foreign investors as the most significant barrier to investment in Korea. The survey results showed that 83 per cent of respondents nominated this as the greatest obstacle (*KED* October 30 1992).

Foreign investors were particularly critical of the government's vacillations concerning the opening of service industries. On the one hand agreements appeared to have been made to open the service market (East Asian Executive Reports Jan 1990) but on the other bureaucrats appeared to be unwilling to approve investment in these industries. In 1990 a Hong Kong Bank survey of the investment environment of various Asian countries reported that Korea was not really interested in foreign investment and that self sufficiency was being pushed harder than ever (*KED* Sept 4 1990). In 1992 a foreign investor was reported to have said that while US pressure was forcing Korea to open up some areas, mid level bureaucrats continued to be able to decide 'what the fatherland should or should not have' (*Asian Business* April 1992: 47).

Foreign investors also complained about what seemed to be discrimination against them. In 1991 it was reported that the office of national tax administration would be carrying out audits of foreign operations to ensure that a 'proper' amount of tax was paid (*KED* July 8 1991). Following press coverage of protests by Koreans against opening the domestic market to foreign retailers (*Business Korea* July 1990: 74–6), the Ministry of Trade and Industry issued an instruction to local bureaus to ensure that foreign retailers were abiding by the strict terms of the operating conditions (*KED* July 1 1991). These included a maximum space for each store and a limited number of outlets.

The unsatisfactory outcomes from both the point of view of the free market advocates and that of foreign investors is evident from the statistics relating to foreign investment shown in Table 5.1. While the 1986–88 period saw significant increases over the 1979–85 period, investment performance since 1989 remained at around US $ 800 million annually, if a single large investment in the petroleum industry in 1991 is excluded. Part of the reason has to be attributed to a continuation of the government's restrictive policies. Thus, overall growth in investment tended to be sluggish particularly in comparison to the boom that was occurring in investment in South East Asia.

The industrial distribution of foreign investment is also shown in Table 5.1. It shows that the manufacturing sector continued to dominate investment flows given the limited ability of foreign firms to invest in the service sector. Within manufacturing industries, electronics and chemical industries showed the strongest performance. In the electronics sector, the surge in investment in 1986–88 was due to a further wave of Japanese companies relocating to Korea to take advantage of lower wage costs and to avoid the effects of the appreciating yen. Joint venture arrangements were entered into between such companies as Samsung and Toshiba and Goldstar and Hitachi to manufacture VCR's for the export market. This Japanese investment began to flow from 1986 before the industrial unrest and wages explosion which occurred in late 1987. The magnitude of this investment is reflected in the fact that prior to 1986 nearly a third of Japan's investment was in the hotel sector with only 12 per cent in the electronics sector. By the middle of 1987, electronics investment had shot up to account for 45 per cent of Japanese investment entering Korea at that time (*Business Korea* June 1988: 26). Investment in these industries declined as from 1989 as increasing costs in Korea led Japanese companies to turn to ASEAN countries for lower cost production (*Business Korea* July 1990: 74–6). The consolidation of investments by Ford and GM in the car industry, as well as an upsurge in parts makers to

Table 5.1: Foreign Direct Investment by Industry (1986–92) (US million dollars)

Industry	1986	1987	1988	1989	1990	1991	1992	1986–92 $	%
Agriculture Livestock, Fishery	3	2	11	2	5	–	–	23	0.4
Mining	1	–	1	–	1	–	2	5	0.1
Manufacturing	242	375	559	504	596	941	605	3822	67.2
Fibre/Garment	6	10	15	16	7	18	14	85	1.5
Timber and Paper	–	–	8	9	7	9	3	38	0.7
Food	18	39	27	38	30	16	108	227	4.9
Chemical	15	45	89	121	145	180	229	824	14.5
Medicines	19	24	47	13	32	56	30	221	3.9
Fertilisers	–	–	–	–	–	–	–	–	–
Petroleum	–	12	–	–	37	395	2	446	7.8
Ceramic	8	6	7	7	15	14	54	111	2.0
Metals	2	7	14	12	5	3	23	65	1.1
Machinery	17	26	72	66	84	112	47	424	7.5
Electric/Electronic	39	158	222	110	88	107	57	782	13.8
Transport Equip	112	38	43	105	140	24	34	495	8.7
Other manufactures	5	10	17	8	4	8	2	54	0.9
Services	231	249	323	306	293	236	196	1834	32.3
Finance	6	17	86	49	157	72	46	432	7.6
Insurance	–	1	6	51	19	44	44	164	2.9
Construction	–	9	–	–	–	2	–	11	0.2
Transport/Storage	–	1	1	–	5	2	1	10	0.2
Hotels	217	213	215	176	65	36	9	933	16.4
Wholesale and Retail	2	–	1	1	1	5	11	21	0.4
Trading	–	–	6	20	28	53	55	163	2.9
Restaurants	–	–	2	1	–	3	11	18	0.3
Others	5	10	6	7	18	20	20	86	1.5
Total	477	626	894	812	895	1177	803	5684	100.0

Source: Ministry of Finance 1993: 291, Table 6–25

supply the newly promoted auto industry contributed to the continuing good performance of the transport equipment sector. A single large investment by the Dutch Aramco company in joint venture with Sanyong accounts for almost all of the investment in the petroleum industry at the time.

While MacDonalds was able to get special permission to open an outlet in the restricted restaurant sector in 1986 (*Business Korea* Sept 1986: 91), only minor investment in most other areas of the service market including wholesale and retail, restaurants transport and construction. The only service industries demonstrating a significant level of foreign participation were finance and hotels. The investment in hotels occurred predominantly in the 1986–88 period leading up to the Seoul Olympics and included a single US $300 million investment by the Lotte group for the expansion of its Seoul hotel facilities (*Business Korea* Sept 1986: 91).

Although foreign investors responded to the lifting of joint venture restrictions by increasing their level of ownership in those industries where this occurred such as pharmaceuticals (*KED* June 17 1991), overall levels of wholly foreign owned investment grew only slowly. The percentage of investment projects proceeding with 100 per cent foreign equity increased from 9.8 per cent to 22.7 per cent by number but only from 22 per cent to 28.1 per cent in terms of total investment amount (MOF 1993: 292). This suggests that smaller manufacturing investments which presented no real threat to Korean firms were allowed to be 100 per cent owned but larger scale projects were still required to have a joint venture partner.

The continuing restrictive approach is also evident from the relatively low number of cases proceeding by way of the automatic approval system. Table 5.2 shows that the percentage of foreign investment projects utilising the automatic approval system remained at around 20 per cent. This is similar to the figures for the 1984–87 period.

It has been noted that in previous periods foreign investment had assumed little significance in total foreign capital inflows due to the state's preference for loans to finance development. The situation began to change as from 1986 as shown in Table 4.2. Foreign investment increased its share of capital inflow rising from 16 per cent in 1986 to 32 per cent in 1988. In 1990, foreign investment surpassed foreign loans for the first time amounting to 66 per cent of foreign capital inflow. However, while this appears to represent a greater reliance on foreign investment as a source of foreign capital, it needs to be balanced against the role that the stock market played as a drawcard for foreign funds. The run down in loans may well have been in anticipation of its opening to foreign participation in 1992. In 1992 alone some US $2 billion in foreign capital entered Korea via the stock market and amounts have increased since that time. As Table 4.2 shows, this figure is significantly higher than the combined total of loans and direct foreign investment.

It is now necessary to turn to the reasons for the state's lack of capacity to introduce policy reforms which would improve the investment performance in line with the objectives of those who, in the early years of the Roh administration, advocated a more liberal approach.

Table 5.2: Investment Approvals by way of Automatic Approval/Notification (1987–92)
(Unit: US million dollars; number of cases)

Year	By Delegated bank		Total		Per cent	
	Cases	Amount	Cases	Amount	Cases	Amount
1987	50	16.7	362	1063.3	13.8	3.0
1988	118	49.0	343	1283.8	34.4	4.0
1989	91	48.2	336	1090.3	27.1	4.5
1990	75	45.6	296	802.6	25.3	5.7
1991	49	57.6	286	1396.0	17.1	4.1
1992	39	67.8	233	894.5	16.7	7.5

Source: MOF 1995(c): 4–5

Roh Tae Woo and State Capacity

The state's ability to autonomously formulate and implement economic policy began to erode from about 1980 but more significantly from 1987 when the democracy movement swept Chun Doo Hwan from power. The increased move towards democratisation also meant that the debate concerning economic policy direction now widened from within the state to encompass groups outside of it.

External actors added weight to the case for a more market oriented foreign investment policy. There was also some support for this from big business. However, the newly democratised environment increased the need for the incumbent regime to attempt to maintain broad cross sectional support. Deregulatory measures would not have enhanced its position in this regard. Consequently societal pressures together with the institutional arrangements existing within the state resulted in insignificant policy change in the direction desired by the free market advocates.

Until the mid 1980s, Korean policy makers had been able to insulate themselves from external pressure for change due in large measure to the willingness of the United States to accept a trade deficit because of Korea's significance to the western alliance as a front line state. From about the mid 1980s, the United States under the Reagan administration began to pressure countries which had large trade surpluses with them to reduce barriers to allow greater access for US companies both by way of trade and investment. In September 1985, the President of the US had directed an investigation into the Korean insurance industry pursuant to section 301 of the Trade Act. This was followed by investigations into the distribution of cinema films in October 1985 and requests by the US in 1987 for the opening of sea transport, warehousing, freight forwarding and advertising to foreign participation (Young S.G. 1988: 61).

Significant external pressure for policy change began after the fall of the Chun regime in 1987. A new administration in the United States and signs that the old cold war order was coming to an end began to change the tolerant attitude that previous US administrations had shown to Korea's protectionist policies. While the United States continued to emphasise security issues in its foreign policy especially as far as Korea was concerned, these had come to be balanced to an increasing extent against economic issues.

In 1988, a series of meetings were held between the US and Korean governments to seek further opening of the Korean market. The US meanwhile had passed amendments to the Trade law (Super 301) which would allow it to impose penalty tariffs on goods from countries which were judged not to be giving fair access to US companies. An agreement was reached in 1989 pursuant to which Korea was to take action to address the closed service market (Noland 1992: 11). This not only involved the opening of service sectors for foreign investment but also the abolition of performance requirements and screening mechanisms.

In late 1991 United States' representatives continued to argue that the service sector and in particular the financial services sector remained closed to foreign firms. The Korean government's response was that economic conditions did not allow further opening of it at that time (*Business Korea* Oct 1991: 36–7).

The US was not the only source of external pressure. The diversification of investment in Korea away from Japanese and US dominance towards a greater share for Europeans meant wider international interests were pressuring the Korean government for policy change. Investment in both manufacturing and service industries began to attract considerable investments from Europe for the first time during the 1986–92 period with European investors accounting for nearly a third of foreign investment by the end of the period (MOF 1993). The upward trend of European investment can be explained by a number of factors including the relatively late entry of European firms into the Korean market and the consequent catchup, as well as a desire on the part of Korea to diversify its sources of foreign investment to avoid dependence on Japan and the USA, particularly in technology (MOF 1993: 607). In addition, the ending of the cold war and with it the decline of old pacific alliance systems as determinants of trade and investment flows, and the emergence of a democratic regime in Korea in 1987 improved the perception of European investors of the political climate.

External pressures for the removal of restrictions gained some support from domestic interest groups. The Federation of Korean Industries began to campaign actively for a deregulated economic environment. Its motivation for doing so stemmed from the actions which both Chun and Roh had taken against the chaebol in order to gain some measure of legitimacy for their regimes (Moon 1994: 146–7). In the Chun era these measures had included attempts to force the chaebol to dispose of unused real estate, rationalise their investments in the heavy and chemical industries (Kim E.M. 1988: 117–19; Jung J.K. 1988: 72–3) and sell their non essential subsidiaries (Moon 1994: 148; Koo and Kim 1992: 142). The Roh administration again attempted to force the chaebol to sell off unused real estate, specialise in certain areas of business activity and proposed the implementation of a real name financial transaction system to reduce the extent of the underground economy through which many chaebol families had allegedly profited greatly (Moon 1994 154–6; Lee and Lee 1992: 16; *Business Korea* Nov 1988: 37).

In both regimes the state sought to use its control over finance and the extensive licensing system for business activity to compel the chaebol to comply with these policies (Lee and Lee 1992: 15; Moon 1994). Many of the policies ostensibly aimed to reduce the chaebol's dominance in the economy (Moon 1994: 147) in order to be seen to be taking some action in response to popular perceptions of the chaebol's economic might being responsible for inequalities in income and wealth distribution (Janelli 1993: 82–3; Lee and Lee 1992: 16). The chaebol actively campaigned for deregulation to rid the state of the power to use such measures claiming that they constituted unwarranted interference in their normal business operations.

As Chairman of the FKI for 10 years, Chung Ju Yung had actively campaigned for greater freedom in business activity. In an interview in 1985 he argued strongly for deregulation of the financial system, an end to the government's centralised credit management and for a firm schedule of market liberalisation to open the economy (*Business Korea* Oct 1985: 18–19). In his last report to the association he argued for 'the government to rationalise all pertinent laws and regulations to develop a system wherein the private sector could do its best to promote business and ensure a laissez faire system' (*Business Korea* March 1987: 22). The successor to Chung, Koo Cha Kyung, Chairman of the Lucky Goldstar group, suggested that his most important task was 'to work for the realisation of a laissez faire system so that business can be freely managed' (*Business Korea* March 1987: 25). The newly appointed senior managing director of the organisation, echoed these views in 1988 when he said 'my focus is to foster an economy run by private industry and not by government' (*Business Korea* July 1988: 94).

The state was placed in a difficult position as a result of the chaebol's' pressure for deregulatory measures. On the one hand, to accede to the chaebol's requests would have resulted in reduced ability to take action against them in the interests of maintaining public support (MacIntyre 1990: 18). On the other hand, continuing high levels of regulation placed constraints on economic activity which ran the risk of reducing the overall growth potential of the economy given the chaebol's' position of structural dominance. The over leveraged position of the chaebol and the dependence of the banking sector on their continued profitability (*Business Korea* Nov 1989: 22–3; Clifford 1994: 310) also constrained the state in the measures that it could take (Kim Y.H. 1994: 54).

The state's dilemma was further complicated by the symbiotic relationship which had developed between state and chaebol whereby particularistic advantages had been given to them in exchange for the huge amounts of funding required for the conduct of election campaigns (Moon 1994: 155; *FEER* March 1 1990: 48; *Business Korea* June 1987: 72–3). To deregulate would have left the state with no mechanisms available to secure this financial support should it not be forthcoming on a voluntary basis.

Differences between free market advocates and interventionists within the state as to the economic desirability of the various measures taken to reduce the chaebol's concentration exacerbated the difficulty that the state had in formulating a coherent response. Reformers took the position that a free market economy would improve the competitive environment in which the chaebol operated thereby leading to greater efficiency and output. Interventionists were concerned about loss of control over economic direction of the economy. For example, it was reported in 1988 that a split had occurred within the Ministry of Trade and Industry between those who favoured a rapid pace of reform and those who favoured continuing government intervention in the interests of the continuation of a coherent industry policy (*Business Korea* Aug 1988: 30).

The state was therefore faced with a number of constraints in acceding to the chaebol's demands for a deregulated economy. On the other hand the chaebol, while publicly advocating deregulation through the FKI, limited this to those policies which sought to restrain their economic activity and not to those policies which provided assistance measures. A good illustration of their seemingly contradictory position can be seen in their opposition to the state's attempt to rationalise the automobile and electricity generating industries in the early 1980s (Kim E.M. 1988: 117–18), yet their willingness to accept very generous incentive packages to take over many financially troubled firms in the mid 1980s to expand their business empires (Moon 1994: 147). The chaebol actively opposed the proposed scaling back of assistance measures in the early years of the Roh administration. The Daewoo group, for example, complained about the government's refusal to give them the assistance they requested for restructuring their shipbuilding operation (*Business Korea* Mar 1989: 33). Again in 1990, the chaebol were said to have actively campaigned for the replacement of Roh's economic team with one that would lift the credit restrictions and restore incentives (Moon 1994: 151; *Business Korea* Apr 1990: 29).

Amsden and Euh (1993: 380) refer to this contradictory position suggesting that the chaebol were keen to preserve the protection of cheap credit while at the same time demanding that the government not use finance to restrict their operations. Eun Mee Kim (1993: 230) suggests that the chaebol wanted a 'protectionist government — one that protected the private sector without heavy handed control'.

Thus the general deregulatory pressure by the chaebol fell far short of advocating in practice the economic liberalisation desired by the free market advocates. The political limitations of the regime's move towards deregulation together with the chaebol's contradictory position allowed lower level bureaucrats the flexibility to resist it in specific areas such as foreign investment policy. Their position was reinforced by other societal pressures which opposed deregulation both generally and on this specific issue.

In the newly democratised environment, the government began to face pressure from the national assembly regarding liberalisation. The domination of the national assembly between 1988 and 1990 by opposition parties made it more difficult for the free market advocates in Roh's government to translate their policy objectives into law (*Business Korea* Aug 1988: 29). Even after the 1990 merger of 2 of the 3 opposition parties with Roh's Democratic Justice Party to form the Democratic Liberal Party, the national assembly continued to place difficulties in the way of reform. The new governing party in the national assembly were able to place pressure on the executive to abandon radical reform through the joint party consultative committee (Haggard and Moon 1990: 215; Moon and Prasad 1994: 365).

The governing party's unwillingness to embrace too much reform arose out of the effects that it would have had on their constituents. Deregulatory measures posed greater competitive pressures on small and medium sized businesses leading to organisations representing them to take their case to the national assembly and the press. This meant that the opposition to liberalisation which had previously been mainly confined to major elements within the bureaucracy was widened to include members within Roh's Democratic Liberal Party. This was most apparent when lobbying occurred among national assembly members of the governing party for the replacement of Roh's economic team with one that would return to the more popular interventionist policies of the past (*Business Korea* Mar 1990: 45). The chairman of the ruling party's special economic committee became the new Deputy Prime Minister for the EPB.

Other societal groups also opposed deregulatory measures which sought to open the economy to foreign competition. This was particularly evident in the protest which occurred during the gradual opening of the Korean market to US goods and services. Numerous examples can be given of a growing anti American mood from within and outside of the bureaucracy because of US pressures. Official signs were posted in subway cars highlighting the dangers to health caused by foreign cigarettes (Janelli 1993: 74–5). Customs officials interpreted customs regulations narrowly to restrict the import of US goods. Some businesses even took steps to prevent the sale of foreign consumer goods which they had earlier imported (Clifford 1994: 308; *FEER* 1990: 40). More public outbursts of anti American sentiment occurred such as the raiding and burning of the US broadcast building in 1990 (Lee M.W. 1990). It was not only the US which was subjected to outbursts of nationalistic fervour. In 1989, a protest rally was held at the Uruguay embassy against the market opening which was being forced upon Korea by the GATT round. Protesters attributed this to the Uruguan government.

The bureaucracy were able to utilise the actions of these societal groups who opposed reform to further their own cause. By opening only those industries that the US demanded be opened they were able to convey the impression that the US was driving the liberalisation process which in turn deflected public criticism away from the bureaucracy and onto the US.

The labour movements approach to foreign investment illustrates the extent of the public's anxiety concerning foreign influences. Between 1987 and 1989, some 200 foreign firms left Korea (Moon and Kim forthcoming: 24) causing not only a loss of jobs but in some cases without meeting existing obligations to employees of back pay and other severance pay. The labour movement responded by the formation of a special union for employees of foreign firms. It called upon the government to continue to scrutinise the activities of foreign firms closely and in particular drafted a proposed amendment to the Foreign Capital Inducement Law to provide compensation for workers when foreign firms relocated. Some spokespersons for the labour movement were reported as suggesting that the government should be much more careful in scrutinising potential foreign investors (*Business Korea* May 1989: 21–2). Actions such as these may well have placed indirect pressure on Roh's administration to slow the pace of liberalisation.

Roh also introduced changes to policy making processes to conform with his more democratic approach (Gibney 1992: 94–5). These institutional changes together with the continuing division within the state between free market advocates and interventionists further weakened the potential for radical policy change.

At the commencement of his term of office Roh enunciated the goals his administration as being democratisation, liberalisation and internationalisation (*Business Korea* Nov 1988: 36). His initial appointments of leading free market economists from Seoul National University to the portfolios of Deputy Prime Minister for the Economic Planning Board and Ministry of Trade signalled an intention to move further towards this position (Rhee 1994: 235). Both Cho Soon as EPB Minister and Han Seung Soo as Trade Minister were reported as having strong ideological views about the free market direction that the economy should take (*Business Korea* March 1989: 33; *Business Korea* March 1991: 16). The initial mood of the administration was captured by Bohn Hoo Koo, the president of the KDI, who said that while the government had played a leading role in economic development in the past, the sixth republic under Roh Tae Woo should be privately led (*Business Korea* June 1988: 47). However, at the same time the free market advocates in the government seemed to be prepared to accept the restrictions that the Roh government sought to impose on the chaebol for legitimacy reasons. In this sense they set themselves up for a confrontation with big business interests. While the chaebol wanted deregulation of controls over private business activity but the continuation of government incentives, the reformers advocated the abolition of incentives yet, in deference to Roh and legitimacy concerns, the imposition of controls.

Roh's decision to significantly decrease the influence that the presidential office (Chong Wa Dae) and its economic secretaries had held over economic policy direction in favour of a greater role for the individual ministers in economic policy making boosted the power that ministers had to push their own views and made it more difficult to reconcile competing positions (*Business Korea* April 1991: 28). In the early years of his term, Roh was also reported as taking a back seat in economic matters concentrating instead on international affairs (Kim E.M. 1993: 280) thereby leaving no effective arbiter of disputes at the ministerial level. Further the EPB's role as a coordinating agency came to be increasingly questioned in the late 1980s (*Business Korea* Aug 1991:

18–19; *Business Korea* Oct 1988: 24) thereby reducing its relative power in relation to other ministries and its ability to resolve policy conflicts between them.

These difficulties at the top left lower level bureaucrats with considerable freedom to formulate policies in their own interest and on what they perceived to be the interests of their constituents. The overall ideologically protectionist views of the lower level bureaucrats were reinforced by a continuing decline in morale. As Sohn Jie Ahn put it:

> The generation of economic technocrats who created the Korean economic miracle in the 1960s and 1970s did not need high salaries and plush working conditions to keep them in the government. But the high morale and pride that was the backbone of any economic technocrat in those days is hard to find today (*Business Korea* July 1992: 17).

This was caused primarily by the perceived threat to their previously powerful positions because of pressure for liberalisation. In addition, longer working hours and less pay than their colleagues in private enterprise strengthened their resolve to salvage their prestige (Evans 1995: 239; *Business Korea* July 1992: 16–19).

In the case of foreign investment policy, while the government sought to respond to US demands, bureaucrats were able to interpret those demands narrowly and respond on a case by case basis rather than within an overall spirit of a more liberal approach. The changes which Roh made to his cabinet in 1990 reinforced the position of the interventionists within the bureaucracy. The return to government intervention to reactivate economic growth significantly lessened the pressure from the top for liberalisation. It allowed lower level bureaucrats to continue to pursue the interests of their constituents for the protection of their own positions as well as because of their continuing belief in the necessity of an interventionist state. Clifford noted how 'on a variety of issues including tobacco, insurance, agricultural products, foreign investment and financial services, South Korea seems to have backed away from the more liberal trade stance it displayed in 1989' (*FEER* July 19 1990: 40).

A further cabinet reshuffle by Roh in March 1991 demonstrated that there would be no return to academic free market economists dominating the economic ministries (*Business Korea* Mar 1991: 16). There was also some relief for the government from the pressure which the FKI had been applying regarding deregulation. The successor to Koo Cha Kyung, not being the head of a major conglomerate, was reputedly far less vigorous in pursuing the outspoken line for less government control (*Business Korea* Mar 1991: 17). Frustrated with the continuing government intervention in private economic concerns, Chung Ju Yung decided to run for president motivated at least in part by the excessive state controls over the economy which had led to his personal humiliation in having to face public examination over Chun's corrupt practices (Yang G. H. 1995: 87–8).

Conclusion

The period of Roh Tae Woo's presidency was characterised by cross currents of internal societal demands and external pressures for change. The institutional arrangements proved to be inadequate in resolving the conflicting viewpoints on the issues raised including that of deregulation generally and liberalisation of foreign investment in particular.

Despite significant external pressure for a more market oriented approach, which attracted some support from big business interests, the state was unable to make any significant progress on the deregulation issue. Not only was there societal opposition as expressed through the national assembly, public demonstrations and through the labour movement, but more significantly the internal dissent over economic policy direction within the state itself continued to make policy change difficult.

The issue of foreign investment provides a good illustration of the difficulties faced in the newly democratised environment. In the mid to late 1980s the United States applied considerable pressure for deregulation on this issue. Big business supported this through its push for a more deregulated economic environment. However inconsistencies in the position of big business on the deregulation issue considerably lessened the impact of their rhetoric. On the other hand, the labour movement advocated the maintenance of strict supervision over foreign firms in the interests of its own members and national assembly representatives, sensing public opposition, advocated less rather than more reform. Roh's party in the National Assembly tended to be opposed to rapid reform because of the impact that this would have on members' constituents and hence their own positions.

The reformers who were appointed by Roh at the commencement of his term were removed from office in a major turn around in policy at the beginning of 1990 thereby slowing the momentum for policy change. While attitudes within the bureaucracy had begun to show some change towards the end of the regime, the entrenched stance of protectionist elements resulted in reform only being carried out in accordance with specific demands by the United States for the opening of specific industries rather than more general deregulation. The institutional arrangements of the state under Roh further weakened the potential for resolution of conflicts concerning economic policy matters with a considerably reduced role for both the EPB and the Blue House in this regard.

The attempt to return to the growth oriented policies of the Park era vindicated those elements of the bureaucracy who had withstood the reformers calls for a more open economy. By the end of the regime few advances had been made in this direction as exemplified by the outcomes of foreign investment policy.

6 Kim Young Sam and the New Foreign Investment Policy Regime

Introduction

The present Korean government has placed foreign investment policy change high on its agenda of economic reform. Kim Young Sam has demonstrated a significant level of interest in this issue which has assisted considerably in the implementation of changes leading to a more market oriented policy.

The elevation of policy concerns to the presidential level together with institutional changes and the increasing acceptance within relevant parts of the bureaucracy of the need for more market oriented policies have been the main factors enhancing the state's bureaucratic capacity for policy change. There has also been considerable internal support and external pressure for the government's policies of internationalisation of the economy and associated deregulatory measures. At the same time, an attempt to carry society along with the state's goal of internationalisation, has meant that much of the opposition to the deregulation of foreign investment has been able to be overcome.

However, there remains a view within the bureaucracy that more needs to be done by the state than leaving foreign investment allocation to market forces. In previous regimes, such a view tended towards the protection of Korean industries from foreign competition. While there is still some evidence that this current of opinion remains, the main debate in the foreign investment arena has concerned the extent to which incentives should be provided to attempt to attract foreign investment in high technology industries.

This chapter reviews the environmental setting in which policy has been formulated. It then proceeds to examine the changes that have been made in the context of their movement towards what has been earlier defined as a free market approach. The debate concerning continuing state intervention is then canvassed within the context of the further development of technological capability. Finally the underlying capacity of the state in relation to this issue is addressed.

The Policy Environment 1993–95

The period since 1993 has been characterised by an environment in which international economic issues have moved to the top of the international agenda. Among these developments, the conclusion of the GATT Uruguay round, the moves to increase the rate of integration in the EEC, the formation of the North American Free Trade Association and the Asia Pacific Economic Cooperation Forum (APEC) as well as Korea's joining the Organisation for Economic Cooperation and Development (OECD) have pushed international economic concerns to the forefront of the agenda for domestic policy makers (Kim C.O. 1995). The tenor of the new international economic order has been one which has very much favoured the position of the free market advocates within the Korean state.

The new GATT agreement requires member countries to give greater access to their markets particularly in agricultural goods and in services (Chung J.Y. 1995: 31–5). These are areas where Korea has traditionally been highly protectionist. The APEC forum, in which Korea is keenly participating, envisages going beyond the significant liberalisation of the new GATT accord with members of APEC further reducing trade and investment barriers amongst themselves and to the rest of the world. Additionally Korea's recent membership of the OECD requires it to have similar rules for access to its markets as other countries within the organisation. The organisation has a series of committees which investigate membership proposals to ensure that member countries regulations conform to OECD norms. The requirements of all of these international bodies has propelled policy makers in Korea towards a more market oriented position in relation to trade and investment.

There is considerable evidence that the Kim administration considers that the best way forward for Korea is to pursue a more open market policy. Kim has personally adopted the slogan of globalisation and internationalisation in order to attempt to convince Koreans of the need to open to the outside world in order to continue the country's economic development. His initial appointment of economic reformers to the posts of Minister for the Economic Planning Board, the Ministry of Finance, Ministry of Trade and the Prime Ministership showed a recognition of the need to pursue the market oriented line more quickly (*Business Korea* March 1993: 16–18). In a major shake up of ministerial positions in December 1993, Kim retained his Ministers of Finance and

Trade as well as his chief economic secretary to maintain the consistency of his reform efforts (*Business Korea* Jan 1994: 17) Despite a further turnover of ministers following the major reorganisation of government administration at the end of 1994, Kim retained Hong Jae Hyun who, as Minister of Finance, had been a key figure in the foreign investment reforms. Hong was promoted to the new post of Minister for Finance and Economy which was a merger of the old EPB and Ministry of Finance. This merger together with the appointment of Hong as the first Minister of the new department signalled a strong intention to continue the reform strategy.

Kim Young Sam also retained persons who were sympathetic to a market oriented approach as his chief economic advisers both before and after assuming the presidency. Prior to assuming the presidency, Kim's chief economic adviser and personal economics tutor was Han Lee Hun who had a prior career in the EPB. He later moved to head the Fair Trade Commission where he indicated his intent a move to strengthen competitive forces within the Korean economy (*Business Korea* May 1993: 21–2). Kim's chief economic secretary Park Jae Yoon was also noted as having advocated economic reform in his previous position of Professor of Finance at Seoul National University (*Business Korea* March 1993: 16–17). Kim's powerful influence in the Democratic Liberal Party also ensured party support for his deregulation policies.

The pro reform ideology of the state elite has been supported by significant organisations representing both local and foreign business. In early 1993, Chey Jong Hyun, the chef executive of the Sunkyong group assumed the leadership of the Federation of Korean Industries. He immediately advocated a much less interventionist role for government arguing that the economy had reached a level of maturity that necessitated a withdrawal of government from the private economic activities of citizens. He indicated an intent during his term to work to promote the interests of free competition in the Korean economy and expressed support for the administration's push for general deregulatory measures cautioning however that it would not be an easy task (*Business Korea* March 1993: 24–5).

Organisations which represent the interests of foreign investors have placed pressure on the administration for reform. In 1994, the American Chamber of Commerce in Korea released a report which was highly critical of foreign investment policies and the investment environment. It cited major obstacles to foreign investment being the lack of transparency of regulation, the failure of lower level bureaucrats to implement policies announced at the top and an overly hierarchical bureaucracy obsessed with red tape (AmCham 1994: 7–12). Similarly in 1994, the European Chamber of Commerce released its report which echoed many of the recommendations of the American Chamber of Commerce (ECC 1994: 88). The recommendations of these reports were further supported by some of the findings of the Swiss based International Institute for Management Development which in its study of the international competitiveness of 41 countries rated Korea 25th overall but 30th in terms of the policy environment. While this reflected the overall highly regulated Korean economy, it was also an indictment of foreign investment policy which by many measures had remained highly regulated well into the 1990s.

Kim Young Sam has also shown significant personal commitment to a more market oriented foreign investment policy. On a number of occasions he is reported to have pledged to make Korea one of the best places in the world for foreigners to do business (*Financial Post* May 28 1994; AmCham 1994: 7) and to open it up to foreign investment (*Business Korea* Dec 1993: 22; *Reuters* March 9 1995). At the same time the administration has been prepared to recognise that one of the major difficulties in doing so are the traditional protectionist attitudes which still pervade parts of the bureaucracy. Nearly a decade earlier Kim Ki Hwan had been severely criticised for voicing criticism of government officials. In December 1993 Kim Young Sam echoed these criticisms when he indicated that bureaucratic processes were placing hindrances in the way of Korea's attempt to induce foreign capital and technology (*FEER* Dec 9 1993: 5) and that some government officials lacked the international awareness needed for a post Uruguay round world (*Business Korea* Jan 1994: 17). The point was made more strongly by Deputy Prime Minister Lee when he said that government officials needed to change their mindset away from the traditional exclusionist thinking of the past and stop discrimination against foreign business concerns if Korea was to induce the foreign capital and technology that it needed (*Business Korea* Dec 1993: 23). The author of the article followed up the point by adding that it was common knowledge that middle level officials in the bureaucracy were a very different breed from the Western educated top ranking government officials who advocated an open market economy.

Towards a Market Oriented Solution—Foreign Investment and Sectoral Opening

The first major policy initiatives of the Kim Young Sam government to liberalise foreign investment in line with a more market oriented approach occurred within the first few months of his term. On June 26, 1993 a timetable was announced for the opening of many of the sectors which had previously been restricted for foreign investors. In this context opening meant the removal of a particular field of business activity from the restricted list with the effect that there remained no special conditions imposed on foreign investors investing in that industry. The plan had been prepared by the foreign investment division of the Ministry of Finance in consultation with other ministries. The opening of the various restricted areas was to take place over the following five years. A number of industries were opened on 30 June 1993 and various groups of industries were scheduled for opening on the first of January in each of the years through 1994–97. An examination of the types of industries to be released in each year is useful because it assists in explaining the patterns of investment that have occurred since that time.

The official published version of the 1993 plan (MOF 1994(a)) scheduled some areas of construction, road transport services, entertainment and personal services for opening in 1994; wholesale and retail trade and medical facilities for 1995; construction support services and some professional services for 1996 and agricultural production, foreign trade, freight services and some aspects of sea and air transport for 1997.

In 1994, this plan was revised as it did not go far enough in meeting the expectations of the foreign investor community. Reports on the foreign investment environment in Korea by both the American Chamber of Commerce and the European Chamber had criticised the 1993 plan as not proceeding quickly enough (AmCham 1994: 7; ECC 1994: 92). This move also followed an official survey of foreign companies in Korea by the Ministry of Trade and Industry in which it was revealed that 74 per cent of companies stated that the major hurdle to commencing business in Korea was the obtaining of relevant licences (*Business Korea* Feb 1994: 36). The result was to move the opening of a number of industries forward in time as well as reducing the list of those that the previous plan had declared would remain closed even after 1997. In particular, some aspects of air transport and freight services were moved forward to 1995 and some aspects of distribution of agricultural products, freight and passenger transport and real estate activities were scheduled for opening in 1996 when previously they had been either not scheduled for opening at all or were scheduled for opening at a later time (MOF 1995).

In 1995, further revisions were made to the plan to open some of the areas which even the 1994 revisions had left closed or restricted and in particular these relate to sections of the transport and communications industries which were either moved forward for opening or were scheduled for partial opening when they had previously been planned to remain restricted. The 1995 revisions seem to have been made because of pressures from the OECD capital issues committee (MOF Sept 1995(a):

3). The overall result of the plans is that when liberalisation is complete only some parts of the media, public transport, insurance and professional service industries will remain closed with some continuing restrictions on parts of air transport, publishing, communications, insurance, real estate services and public utilities (MOF 1995(b)). These changes, if fully implemented, will result in Korea's foreign investment rules being similar to those of other OECD countries

In addition, it was agreed in 1995 that, subject to approval, foreign investment would be able to proceed by way of merger and takeover of existing Korean companies through the purchase of their shares as from 1997 (MOF 1995(a): 4–5). At present, foreign investors are limited to acquiring only 15 per cent of the shares of Korean companies through the stock exchange. The capital issues committee of the OECD was highly critical of such a policy remarking that a country is not open to foreign investment if investment by way of merger and takeover is not permitted (*KED* Oct 28 1994). Consequently, in order to be accepted for membership Korea has had to change this policy.

The second major area of policy change has been in the approvals system. The notification system had been first introduced in 1991 and expanded in 1992 to make it possible for investors to proceed with their investment simply by way of notification to the Bank of Korea unless the investment was in a restricted area or one that required tax incentives in which case approval was needed from the Ministry of Finance. The combination of the notification system together with the market opening schedule has produced the result that as a sector moves off the restricted list in accordance with the government timetable, investors can make an investment in that industry simply by notifying of their intention to do so. In 1994, the Bank of Korea as Korea's central bank was relieved of the duty of accepting all notifications and the authority to accept notifications was given to all major banks who could deal in foreign exchange. In December 1994, a number of foreign banks were added to the list of banks which could accept notifications after some pressure for this from the US Chamber of Commerce.

While the changes to the approval system in combination with the sectoral opening plan have greatly simplified the procedures required for foreign companies to invest in Korea, once inside the country foreign companies must still endure the same highly regulated environment that Korean companies encounter when establishing businesses. When commencing a business, the ordinary Korean company is confronted with a plethora of licensing requirements originating in the various ministries responsible for the field of activity in which they wish to engage. Attempts to deregulate these controls have met with mixed success (Lee S.C. 1995; Kim I.J. 1995). The reasons for this will be discussed later but at this point it may be noted that one of the major stumbling blocks has been inability to shift the position of some parts of the bureaucracy who continue to regard regulation as necessary. In addition foreign investors are still subject to foreign exchange regulations when bringing in capital and accordingly until these regulations are liberalised, some control still exists at this stage of the process.

Because the general deregulation process is likely to be a lengthy one, mechanisms have been put in place to give foreign investors special assistance in dealing with the regulatory requirements which ordinary Korean companies must face. In 1994, the Foreign Capital Deliberation Committee was given authority to deal with any grievances that foreign investors had either with the foreign investment approval process or in obtaining permission to start and operate their business. In addition one stop shops to assist foreign investors in dealing with any aspect of making an investment in Korea were established in downtown Seoul and in fifteen regional locations in June 1995.

While it is yet too early to make a comprehensive assessment of the success of the reform efforts some preliminary indication can be given. Table 6.1 sets out the industrial distribution of foreign investment since 1993.

It can be seen that foreign investment has improved its performance in comparison to the 1989–92 period when it averaged only some US $800 million per year. In 1995 particularly, foreign investment appears to have shown considerable growth to an annual inflow of nearly US $2 billion. This is almost twice the annual inflow of 1993. However, a note of caution is necessary here. The figures produced for the previous periods have been on the basis of investment arrivals. The only figures available for the 1993 to 1995 period are for investment approvals. It is likely that some of the investment approved during this period may not actually eventuate and accordingly the 1993–95 figures need to be viewed with this qualification in mind.

As far as its industrial distribution is concerned, foreign investment in service industries surpassed foreign investment in manufacturing industries for the first time in 1994 and the trend continued in 1995. This seems to reflect the ongoing removal of restrictions in those industries as from the middle of 1993. In the service areas two of the sectors showing strong growth have been wholesale and retail businesses and trading activities. These are two sectors of the Korean economy in which restrictions have been recently lifted under the liberalisation plan and where foreign companies feel that they have some advantages. The first half of 1994, for example, saw 11 major projects approved in the distribution sector as foreign companies moved to establish a market presence in time for the complete opening of the retail market in 1995.

**Table 6.1: Foreign Direct Investment by Industry (1993–95)
(US million dollars)**

Industry	1993	1994	1995	1992–95
Agriculture				
Livestock, Fishery	.1	–	.3	.4
Mining	–	.3	.1	.4
Manufacturing	526.8	401.7	883.4	1812.0
Fibre/Garment	4.6	6.1	58.4	69.9
Timber and Paper	1.6	7.2	83.0	91.8
Food	39.4	17.8	14.8	72.0
Chemical	241.2	106.9	174.4	522.5
Medicines	22.7	38.0	65.2	125.9
Fertilisers	1.2	–	–	1.2
Petroleum	20.7	8.2	44.9	73.8
Ceramic	29.1	27.7	20.3	77.1
Metals	15.1	7.4	7.5	30.0
Machinery	49.8	48.7	101.9	200.4
Electric/Electronic	45.2	63.1	227.9	536.6
Transport Equip	44.1	66.2	72.1	182.4
Other manufactures	12.2	4.3	13.0	29.5
Services	517.3	914.5	1057.5	2489.3
Finance	57.0	293.8	378.2	729.0
Insurance	8.7	8	56.2	72.9
Construction	1.1	6.8	11.8	19.7
Transport/Storage	.6	8.1	3.2	11.9
Hotels	102.7	293.1	216.1	611.9
Wholesale and Retail	63.5	21.7	138.3	223.5
Trading	92.2	101.4	106.8	300.4
Restaurants	35.1	4.3	8.5	47.9
Electricity and Gas	–	26.0	–	26.0
Others	156.5	151.4	138.5	446.4
Total	1044.2	1316.5	1941.3	4302.0

Source: Ministry of Finance 1995(c): 7

Much of this investment aimed at price competitiveness through the opening of discount stores, general merchandising stores and membership warehouse clubs. (*KED* Jan 4 1995).

Other sectors showing a strong performance are finance and hotels. A liberalisation plan was also prepared for the financial sector in 1993 (Dalton 1993) and foreign financial institutions may be taking steps to establish a market presence in anticipation of liberalisation being inevitable because of pressures from the OECD finance committee (KED Oct 28 1994). The considerable investment in hotels in 1995 reflects the increased demand for tourist and business accommodation in Seoul.

In the manufacturing sector, there has been a revival of investment in the electronics and machinery industries in 1995 both in terms of the number of cases and the amount of investment. This may have resulted from the increased ability of foreign firms to sell products on the domestic market through affiliated wholesale and retail chains. In 1994 major electronics companies such as JVC, Sony and Tandy all opened outlets with Phillips being the first foreign company to advertise its electronics products through the television media (*KED* December 1 1994).

The impact of the notification system has become apparent over the past three years. As indicated earlier, between 1984 and 1992 only 20 per cent of investments proceeded via the automatic approval system which was the predecessor of the notification system. The increasing use of the system is reflected in Table 6.2 which sets out investment by way of approval and by way of notification since 1993.

Table 6.2: Investment Approvals by way of Automatic Approval/Notification (1993–95)
(Unit: US million dollars; number of cases)

Year	By Delegated Bank		Total		Per cent	
	Cases	Amount	Cases	Amount	Cases	Amount
1993	82	100.4	273	1044.3	30.0	9.6
1994	199	385.8	414	1316.5	48.0	29.3
1995	492	962.5	555	1941.3	88.6	50.0

Source: MOF 1995: 4–5

It can be seen that by way of numbers of projects the notification system accounted for approximately 30 per cent of investment cases in 1993 rising to nearly 90 per cent in 1995. The percentage of investments by way of amount proceeding by way of notification has also shown a dramatic increase. This indicates the success of the government's efforts to simplify approval procedures.

There is also some tentative evidence of the government's success in changing the mindset of government officials who have been described as discriminating against foreign investment. If foreign investors were experiencing severe difficulties with the secondary tier approvals necessary then it is reasonable that they might seek to utilise the new grievance procedures which have been set up for them. Enquiries revealed that in the first nine months of operation of the one stop shop and the new grievance procedures there had not been a single case of foreign investors referring problems regarding approvals to it. Others, however, are more sceptical and suggest that more conservative bureaucrats have simply adopted the approach that they can wait out the reform minded policies of the current regime (*Business Korea* Jan 1994: 17).

Technology Transfer and Foreign Investment—Remnants of an Interventionist Approach

During the major part of the 1980s the debate between interventionists and free market advocates hinged around the issue of continued protection for Korean industries from foreign competition. Although it had been a major aim of the reformers' liberalisation strategy in the early 1980s to encourage more foreign investment with a view to enhancing the technological capabilities of Korean industries (Haggard and Cheng 1987: 125; Kim C.J. 1988; Chu K.I. 1989: 4; Kim I.H. 1987: 3), technology policy issues became lost in the general industrial restructuring concerns of the early 1980s. In the mid 1980s it may also have been largely overlooked as the economy recovered strongly due to the combination of low oil prices, the low value of the won as compared to the yen against the US dollar and the continuing relatively low wages of Korean workers (*Business Korea* Feb 1991: 41–3). It may also have been the case that the general position of the free market advocates that technology development should be a matter for the market resulted in this issue receiving a low priority among top policy makers. While some impressive strides in technology development were made by a few firms particularly in the semiconductor industry (*FEER* July 19 1984: 64; Evans 1995: 160), leaving technology development to the market alone may have meant a concentration by many business firms on short term profits more than on research and development (*FEER* June 28 1990: 42–5).

A number of circumstances combined in the late 1980s to refocus the attention of policy makers on technology issues. First the rapid increase in labour costs during the 1987–89 period had resulted in a further loss of comparative advantage in labour intensive industries (Cho Soon 1994: 190). Over this period a large number of both foreign and local firms engaged in these industries had relocated their plants to cheaper destinations in South East Asia and China (*Business Korea* July 1990: 74). Such countries were seen to be narrowing the technological gap between themselves and Korea while at the same time Korea remained well behind technological leaders such as Japan and the US in many fields (Cho Soon 1994: 190; Hong 1994: 28). Kim and Dahlman (1992: 441) have pointed out that even in 1992, Korea had few industries which could be said to fall into the category of developing emerging technology. Hong (1994: 34–5) and Nam (1991: 29) also note that Korea lacked self sufficiency in some core technologies and design capability.

In addition there was an imbalance in technological capability between Korea's larger companies and small and medium enterprises (Hong 1994: 34) which continues to exist through to the present time. Evidence of this is the few instances of small and medium firms entering into joint venture or licensing arrangements to acquire advanced technology. While larger companies have demonstrated some prospects of entering into strategic alliances with leading multinational firms for the joint development of new technologies in some areas (Hong 1994: 34), small companies find it more difficult to establish technological linkages. The Small and Medium Industry Promotion Corporation has assistance measures for small and medium firms wishing to establish technology links through licensing or joint venture with foreign firms. However it has been noted by that organisation that foreign firms seem to be more interested in establishing sales outlets rather than licensing or joint venture linkages (*KED* January 16 1993). The technological development of Korea's small and medium firms is seen as a priority because of their significance in industrial production in some industries such as machinery (*Business Korea* February 1993: 26) as well as their role as suppliers of inputs to large firms (*Business Korea* February 1991: 43). Without a technologically advanced small and medium industry sector overall industrial development will suffer (Hong 1994: 34).

As well as these issues of declining cost competitiveness and structural imbalances, there was also concern regarding the increasing difficulty that firms found in obtaining technology through other means such as licensing. In the past Korea had been able to obtain much of its technological capability through informal means such as reverse engineering, copying, sending technicians abroad for training as well as through the formal mechanism of licensing. While informal methods and licensing are appropriate for the adoption of many mature technologies, they are less adequate for the emergent stages of technology development. Foreign firms guard their emerging technologies closely precluding acquisition by informal means. Likewise, they are reluctant to licence advanced technology to Korean companies because of the potential competition that they might pose in the future (Matsuura 1989; Hong 1994: 15).

Additionally, foreign firms were hesitant to invest in Korea in high technology areas unless they were able to be assured of 100 per cent foreign ownership in order to have the maximum chance of protecting and profiting from the ownership advantages they had developed in this area (Kim and Dahlman 1992: 445). Intellectual property protection in Korea has been considered to be weak in the past (*Business Korea* May 1993: 24–6). A survey of the Asian business environment by the Hong Kong bank in 1990 had been reported as commenting that there was no other country in Asia where foreign investors needed to be as careful with their proprietary rights in technology (*Globe and Mail* Toronto September 1994).

All of these factors led to a body of opinion in the late 1980s that in order for it to advance into high technology areas Korea needed to return to policies which encouraged self reliance (*Business Korea* November 1987: 26) more than foreign investment and licensing as mechanisms for technological advancement. There was a substantial body of research which could be called upon to show that policies which emphasised self reliance in technology development had been successful in the past. As noted earlier, this had been the strategy in the Park era except in apprentice industries where the state had policy measures in place to ensure technology transfer.

Kim and Dahlman (1992: 449) noted that past policies of encouraging self reliance through protecting local firms which were developing new technology had led to increasing levels of research and development by those firms. Lee's study (1987) as referred to in Enos (1989: 16) had also found that there was greater potential for technology development in wholly owned Korean companies than in long term joint venture arrangements. Enos also notes that a separate study by himself and Park of the technology development of four firms over time confirmed Lee's findings that 'local effort has been the most significant factor in its success in acquiring technology' (Enos 1989: 18–19).

A survey of some 1700 front line managers of firms in Korea which were technology licensees was conducted by the Korea Industrial Bank in 1991. The survey included both domestic and foreign invested firms and took place by interview of managers to establish how technology transfer had taken place and in what areas. In the analysis of the results, technologies were divided into eight categories consisting of product design technology, parts/material technology, production base technology, manufacturing process technology, equipment maintenance technology, test evaluation technology, production management technology and software technology. The findings specifically mentioned the importance of foreign invested firms in advancing technological capability in production base technology, manufacturing process technology, and equipment maintenance technology (MOF 1993: 395–401). This seems to support the conclusion above that foreign invested firms tend to primarily transfer technology related to improvements in production rather than the higher order activities of design and parts/material technologies.

This is further supported by a study of the computer industry by Linsu Kim (1987) in which he noted the relative lack of foreign participation in the high end of the market. He shows that foreign subsidiaries and joint ventures were mostly engaged in the production of PC's and peripheral computer hardware whereas in the higher value micro and mini computers, it was local firms who dominated. In a further study of automated programmable technology acquisition by Korean firms Kim states that 'direct foreign investment as a mechanism of PA technology transfer is yet few in number, very recent in history and limited mainly to process control equipment and system' (Kim Linsu 1988: 285–6). Programmable automation technologies include such diverse techniques as computer assisted design; computerised machine tools; robotics; automated inspection and testing equipment and process control equipment. It is interesting that foreign investment predominated in only one of these technologies, process control equipment in the 1978–86 period. This tends to confirm the view that foreign investors transfer existing technology oriented to production processes rather than design or innovative capability.

On the basis of these studies it could be concluded that strategies of self reliance are of more value than foreign investment in the development of technological capability in emerging high technology activities. The difficulty for policy makers in pursuing a policy which stressed self reliance alone was that while Korean companies had invested heavily in research and development during the 1960s, 1970s and even into the early 1980s, by the late 1980s levels of research and development expenditure were well below international norms (*Business Korea* Feb 1991: 42–3; *KED* 12 October 1992). The ratio of research and development expenditure to sales was higher in foreign invested firms in Korea than in local firms in the late 1980s (Koo and Bark 1988: 48). Further, by 1987 nearly 50 per cent of all licence agreements in Korea were with foreign invested firms (ibid). This poor performance of local firms led to the prospect that as imperfect as it may be as a source of technology transfer, foreign investment may act as a competitive spur to local companies to develop their own technology as well as providing the best possibility for technology acquisition given the limitations of licensing and informal methods of acquisition.

A number of papers from significant Korean Research Institutes in this area have come to favour this view. In a paper on the topic produced by the Korea Institute for International Economic Policy (KIEP), it was suggested that foreign investment might increase its technology spill over effect through competitive pressures (Byun and Wang 1994: 17). It was noted however that in some cases assistance might be needed to be given to local firms to ensure they were in a position to compete. This confirmed the conclusions of an earlier study by the Korea Institute for Economics and Technology (KIET) of foreign investment in 12 industries over the 1967–88 period. The report concluded that the government should strengthen technology training to take advantage of the technology which could be transferred through foreign investment (*KED* October 28 1991).

The possibility of foreign investment playing a leading role in technology development also appears to have been accepted by top policy makers in the current regime. What is also accepted is the need to simultaneously encourage self reliance. In a speech made to the Foreign Correspondents Club in Seoul on April 7, 1995, the Minister of Trade Industry and Energy, Park Jae Yoon said

> The most critical task in shaping Korea's competitive edge in the world is to raise our technological level so that we can compete more effectively in upscale capital intensive markets. Korean industry is no longer competitive in labour intensive production and cannot close the technological gap through its efforts alone. While the government will continue to expand R&D expenditure, we will actively pursue joint R&D and technological cooperation with major technologically advanced countries. As previously noted our efforts to induce foreign investment will be one of our major means of promoting technological development (*KED* 22 April 1995: 5).

Despite the accepted potential of foreign investment contributing in this way, a number of studies emerged in the 1990s which showed that foreign investment had fallen far short of achieving this potential. A survey by the Bank of Korea in 1991 was undertaken to establish the relative effects of the various modes of technology transfer in a range of industries. The respondents to the survey were allowed 3 choices as to the way in which they had acquired foreign technology. The responses are set out by industry in Table 6.3.

It can be seen that in most industries technology licensing has been the most important vehicle followed by sending engineers abroad and technology training. Foreign investment is relatively less significant in all industry categories. This result is confirmed when the responses for all categories are totalled. The composition of each alternative refers to the percentage of total responses that the specific responses for each category represents. Thus 31.8 per cent per cent of the total responses suggested that firms acquired technology through licensing. On a composite basis foreign direct investment is rather insignificant at 6.5 per cent of total responses and well behind sending engineers abroad, technology training and capital imports. Hong notes that 'many other surveys report similar observations that the role of FDI in technology transfer to Korea has been negligible' (Hong 1994: 4).

Table 6.3: Main channels for Foreign Technology Acquisition

	Licen-sing	Sending engineers abroad	Tech-nology training	Inform-ation associated with capital import	Foreign direct invest-ment	Inform-ation from suppliers	Recruit of over-seas scientists	Others
Electronics	88	66	57	32	15	11	7	0
Electricity	90	71	54	24	20	15	2	10
Machinery	86	66	61	27	18	11	2	5
Chemicals	90	49	53	35	29	10	1	3
Textiles	91	50	63	31	11	12	3	0
Metals	80	61	57	54	20	15	0	0
Ceramics	94	69	50	42	22	8	3	0
Shipbuilding	90	74	74	16	5	11	0	14
Pharma-ceuticals	22	50	46	68	5	9	9	0
Foods	80	50	67	40	7	10	3	0
Average	88	62	58	34	18	11	3	3
Compos-ition	31.8	22.4	20.9	12.3	6.5	4.0	1.1	1.1

Source: Hong 1994: 4, Table 2
Note: Up to three choices were allowed. Composition is the percentage of each average to the total of averages

Further the percentage of overall investment that was of the high technology type had declined from 27 per cent of the total in 1989 to only 12 per cent in 1991 (*KED* February 29 1992). Table 6.4 shows the extent of this decline both in terms of the amount and number investment in high technology industries since 1987. It should be noted that the government produces a specific list of high technology industries. On a number of occasions between 1990 and 1992, this list was expanded, but despite this, investment in the relevant areas declined.

Table 6.4: High-tech Industries in Foreign Investment in Korea 1987–94 (US million dollars; number of cases)

	1987	*1988*	*1989*	*1990*	*1991*	*1992*	*1993*	*1994*
Amount	144	218	255	191	59	58	121	111
Cases	34	23	22	18	14	5	10	15

Source: Ministry of Trade, Industry and Energy
Notes: 1. According to the cases approved or accepted
           2. Total of new and increased investments

The debate between free market advocates and interventionists has centred on the best way of attracting high technology firms and the extent to which special facilities should be provided to them. The view of those favouring a more interventionist approach was that tax incentives should be provided at a generous level as well as special facilities such as high technology parks. A series of proposals were made in 1992 to increase the tax incentives for high technology investment (*KED* May 2 1992), as well as proposals to establish a special park for high tech investors (*KED* Feb 29 1992) and additions to the list of high technology industries eligible for incentives (*KED* Dec 11 1991; *KED* 29 Oct 1992). The response highlights the interventionist line of thinking that there should be attempts to channel foreign investment into high technology industries and that special policy measures were required to achieve this result.

The issue was rekindled in 1994. Editorials in the press suggested that the incentive schemes of South East Asian countries had resulted in increased investment and Korea should follow suit (*KED* July 1 1994) but not to the extent of giving foreign firms preferences over local firms (*KED* June 14 1994) Proponents of this approach included the Korea Institute for Economic and Technology (KIET), the research institute attached to the Ministry of Trade and Industry, which suggested a 7 year tax holiday for high technology firms (*KED* May 25 1994). There was also a widespread view in both the bureaucracy and in private organisations that tax incentives were needed because of the competition for this type of investment. Interviews with government officials indicated that there was general agreement that Korea must continue to offer incentives due to this competition.

The opposing view was that special facilities will not work in attracting high technology investment. Lee's study (1994) is indicative of the market oriented view that the KDI has long held that incentive measures will not be successful in attracting foreign investment. He argued that to attract more foreign investment into Korea, the government should place much more emphasis on improving the level of infrastructure, addressing the difficulties that foreign firms face in obtaining finance and acquiring land, attention to the industrial relations system and intellectual property protection, and making transparent all regulations. He makes the point that in a complex economy the decision made by foreign investors to invest is based on a large range of factors. For the government to attempt to steer foreign investment into selected sectors is no longer feasible or desirable and therefore by implication incentives and restrictions should be abolished.

The depth of difference of opinion on this issue is also highlighted by the conflicting positions of the US and European Chambers of Commerce on the industrial parks issue. In their 1994 report the American Chamber of Commerce stated as follows.

> The Korean government also proposed the establishment of free trade zones with lower land prices for foreign investors. AmCham believes the concept of free trade zones is not appropriate for Korea and is concerned with the manufacturing focus it implies. Korea needs to be a foreign investment country – for all industry sectors (AmCham 1994: 9).

On the other hand, the European Chamber of Commerce had a different view. In their recommendations they stated:

> The government should provide special industrial areas, where land with access to the required utilities is available for purchase or long term lease by new investors (European Chamber of Commerce 1994: 84).

Unlike the case of the opening of sectors which tended to favour the position of the free market advocates, the issue of technology resulted in a policy position much closer to those favouring a more interventionist approach. In December 1994 the government amended the Foreign Capital Inducement law to expand tax incentives from the previous three years with 50 per cent reduction for a further 2 years to 5 years with a 50 per cent reduction for a further 3 years. Tax incentives would apply to investors in a significantly expanded list of high technology areas in which it was considered Korea had a priority for foreign technology. In addition the previous decision of the Roh government to construct two high technology parks for foreign investors has proceeded in order to supply high technology investors with cheap land. Foreign investors in high technology areas are also able to borrow up to 100 per cent of their capital requirements from overseas due to a policy change in 1995 (MOF 1995(a): 1–2). At the same time, action has been taken to strengthen the ability of local firms to benefit by improving self reliance. In 1996, the Science and Technology Policy Institute was established and has as a part of its functions research into policy for international technology cooperation and the provision of financial assistance to local firms for technology development.

The two major areas of foreign investment policy reform have shown a compromise between free market advocates and interventionists. The issue of sectoral opening has favoured the position long advocated by free market advocates for the removal of restrictions whereas that of technology development has tended towards the interventionist position which involves the upgrading of incentives while encouraging self reliance. The ability to arrive at this compromise demonstrates enhanced state capacity to deal with the issue. The features responsible for that are now examined.

Kim Young Sam and State Capacity

The policy changes which the Kim administration has made to foreign investment policy have been possible because of a restoration of state capacity in relation to this issue. This has been possible through strong leadership from top policy makers with support from big business and external actors. The control that Kim exercised over the majority party in the national assembly minimised opposition from this source in the 1993–95 period. At the same time the state has attempted to carry society along with its goals through an appeal to the need for Korea to internationalise and globalise for further economic development.

The more difficult task of dealing with the division within the state concerning this issue has been accomplished through strong leadership as well as institutional reform. Again the government's single minded pursuit of the internationalisation objective has permeated the bureaucracy to the degree that any opposition to issues which are seen to be priorities in fulfilling has not been successful in frustrating reform efforts.

A note of caution is warranted at this point. State capacity varies by issue and over time. While the state has been able to restore its capacity for policy change on the foreign investment issue, this has occurred only through strong leadership on this issue together with specific institutional reforms in relation to it. The lessons from the reform process in this area are that under the current institutional arrangements of the state whereby a hierarchically structured executive arm is almost solely responsible for policy change, reform seems to have to proceed from the top and on an issue by issue basis. Because of the limited time that the leadership has available, this means that many issues must go unaddressed. It might be suggested that the labour issue, environmental issues and infrastructure problems are in this category as well as more thoroughgoing deregulatory measures for the economy at large.

This section proceeds with an analysis of the current regime's political capacity on this issue including its relationship with the big business sector, other societal groups and external actors. It then proceeds to examine the state's enhanced bureaucratic capacity in relation to foreign investment. This includes institutional reform, strong leadership and an increased acceptance of a new ideology of internationalisation.

Under previous regimes the FKI had assumed an increasingly high profile role in pressuring the state for deregulation (Moon 1994, Moon and Kim forthcoming ; Kim I.J. 1995: 172) while at the same time chaebol leaders individually continued to rely on their informal connections with the state based on old school ties, regional associations and kinship groups in obtaining particularistic advantages for specific projects (Weiss 1994; Amsden 1994: 87). As noted earlier, chaebol leaders had also been expected to contribute by way of political donations to the state in exchange for the favours that they had received. Thus while the chaebol supported less government meddling in their affairs, the institutional arrangements which existed between the state and big business dating from the Park era continued to influence state-chaebol interaction on a day to day basis.

At the commencement of the Kim era, state chaebol relations were strained (Choi and Lee 1995). Kim moved against his opponent in the presidential campaign, Chung Ju Yung, with charges of tax evasion. Likewise, Park Tae Joon the former head of POSCO and a previous political opponent of Kim in Kim's race to secure the LDP's party nomination for the presidency (Lee M.W. 1995: 46–7) was removed from his position and pursued on charges of corruption. In addition, legitimacy concerns compelled the regime to be seen to be taking action against what the public had perceived as corrupt practices of the state chaebol relationship (Woo-Cumings 1995: 163–4). The dynamics of this relationship tends to impact adversely on the ability of the state to implement the deregulation required for its internationalisation strategy because as long as the state continues to provide particularistic advantages to large business firms, the arms length relationship which deregulation implies is not be able to be established (*FEER* May 27 1993: 40). In other words the government must be able to sever its old ties of reliance on the big business sector to keep itself in power before general deregulatory measures can be effective. In this respect Kim Young Sam's policy of refusing to dispense favours in exchange for political donations can be seen as an attempt at institutional reform (*Asian Business* June 1993: 30). However recent revelations concerning the Hanbo group seem to suggest that there is still some way to go in changing the nature of state-chaebol interaction.

As far as foreign investment is concerned, big business has long favoured deregulation of the controls over outward investment and accordingly would have placed itself in an inconsistent position by opposing liberalisation of controls over inward investment. There is no evidence of any formal submissions by the FKI on behalf of big business recommending continued controls over inward foreign investment. As has been noted earlier, there has also been significant international pressure on the Kim administration for deregulation of foreign investment. This has coincided with the more general stance of big business groups. In this respect therefore foreign investment policy may well have been easier to deregulate than other areas of economic policy such as control over the financial system.

In addition, Kim was not confronted by countervailing societal pressures on this issue to the same extent as his predecessor thereby making it easier for him to institute change. The lack of effective resistance from other societal groups can in part be attributed to the control over the national assembly by Kim's party and Kim personally during the crucial time of foreign investment policy reform. At the commencement of the current administration, officials of the Democratic Liberal Party indicated strong support for the government's general deregulatory measures (*Business Korea* March 1993: 17) Kim's immense personal popularity and a mandate for reform also assisted. These factors minimised indirect societal pressure on the government through this source.

There is also little evidence of effective opposition to deregulation on this issue from other societal groups including industry bodies. While there were some submissions made by businesses to the Ministry of Finance regarding the liberalisation schedule, the main actors in determining the pace of liberalisation were the Ministries themselves. Enquiries of government officials established that the plan was more a matter of compromise between the various ministries which in turn were supported by opinions from the various research institutes attached to them. It is also likely that in the case of the liberalisation plan, industry associations had little ability or opportunity to block the initiatives. The function of industry associations remains principally one of collecting information requested by the bureaucracy and passing on information from the bureaucracy rather than lobbying.

Additionally, in the case of small firms, while the relevant information concerning the liberalisation plans was passed on to them, it is possible that as these were perceived only as 'plans' and not of immediate consequence to them. They may therefore have been less motivated to attempt to protest directly to the bureaucracy. In the case of the FKI there was little serious discussion between that association and the Ministry of Finance on the issue. It can therefore be concluded that there was little effective societal input into these reforms.

The lack of effectiveness of societal pressure has also been due to the government's attempts to mobilise societal support for a new ideology of internationalisation to replace the previous ideology of development through self reliance. Government campaigns promoting internationalisation in all spheres of life have become commonplace in an attempt to carry society along with the government's goals. Many of the persons interviewed from both private and government agencies expressed the view that there may well be some short term detriment to some Korean firms as a result of liberalisation. However there was widespread agreement that the internationalisation process was both necessary and inevitable given developments in the international economic arena.

The ability of the state to insulate itself from those groups within society who oppose internationalisation has also been considerably assisted through a lack of an institutionalised form of access for them. The example of industry associations has been discussed above. The labour movement provides a further good illustration.

While the labour movement achieved considerable success in improving conditions since 1987 it has failed to establish a unified movement capable of mobilising public support for the direct political participation of labour in the political process. Labour has remained fragmented in its political objectives since 1987. Labour has yet to come up with an alternative strategy for economic development despite the cracks which have appeared within the state concerning the old developmental ideology.

The end of the cold war world order and the failure of the socialist pattern of development have left the traditional objectives of Korean labour movements discredited (Kim B.K. 1995: 25–8). Internal divisions have left large sections of the labour movement disaffected with its potential for political power and many who supported it in the 1987–89 period have now abandoned the cause (Kim and Lim 1994: 3–4) In addition, a ban on direct and indirect linkages between the labour movement and political parties has been continued during the Kim

Young Sam era. Although the stated reason for this has been the priority of continued economic growth, some suggested that the government was more concerned about the possible political implications of the labour movement supporting one of the opposition parties in the 1996 local and congressional elections (Park Y.B. 1993: 581–2).

The relationship between the state and labour has undergone marked shifts during the period since 1980 from outright repression by the state in the Chun Doo Hwan era to an accommodation of labour's broader interests by the present regime. Yet, labour, like small business, still has no significant institutionalised access to policy making processes and in that sense the direct policy influence of labour has changed little since the Park regime (Kim B.K. 1995: 4–5). On the other hand, in the democratised environment since 1987, labour and small business groups have had much greater opportunity to pursue their interests indirectly through attempting to mobilise public support on issues which are of concern thereby making it politically difficult for the government to refuse to respond. Thus it is through this indirect influence rather than through the potential of these groups to directly and effectively lobby policy makers that they can influence policy change. As noted, in the case of foreign investment, the state has successfully used the appeal to internationalisation to minimise this indirect pressure.

It has therefore been the case that in relation to foreign investment policy, the Kim administration has been able to achieve significant change. This has occurred through a combination of lack of opposition from big business and other societal groups, external pressure, Kim's personal commitment to the issue and his control over more general policy making processes. However political capacity alone is insufficient for effective policy change. It has been seen that bureaucratic capacity is equally as important.

The significant change that occurred in foreign investment policy making with the coming to power of the Kim Young Sam government has been that for the first time since Park there has been consistent pressure from the top for policy change. By personally weighing into the debate on foreign investment policy Kim Young Sam has been able to tip the balance in favour of the free market advocates.

The appointment of the ex Minister of Finance as the Deputy Prime Minister for the new Ministry of Finance and the Economy also ensured consistency in policy direction as well as cohesiveness over the crucial stages of the reform process. Kim has shown no reluctance to replace other ministers (Kim B.K. 1995: 39–41) but kept his most senior economic minister, Hong, throughout the 1993–95 period. As a career bureaucrat Hong was well aware of the opposition that existed to market oriented reforms in the past and the difficulties in bringing about effective reform.

A number of institutional changes also occurred in relation to foreign investment. Timetables for liberalisation of finance and foreign investment were prepared early and have, to date, been adhered to. The preparation and publication of these plans in advance of their implementation also made it more difficult for elements in the bureaucracy to block them. As well, Kim has been fortunate in that the group of free market advocates in senior positions in the bureaucracy has been steadily growing since the early 1980s (Amsden 1994) which has meant that there is a significant core of support within the bureaucracy for liberalisation policies.

The Kim government has also sought to reduce bureaucratic resistance to its liberalisation measures in the implementation phase by making some changes to the institutional arrangements for foreign investment. It has done this by appealing to the priorities that the major economic ministries currently have in the economic development agenda. The Ministry of Finance and Economy has been satisfied with the changes because they not only accord with a more free market approach to foreign investment which it has advocated at the most senior levels since the early 1980s but also because it is the Ministry which is under most pressure to liberalise the economy to conform with OECD and Uruguay round requirements. On the other hand those elements within the bureaucracy who believe that more needs to be done than leaving technological change to the free market have also been catered for by the changes.

The Ministry of Trade has been given jurisdiction over the new investment promotion mechanisms which include the establishment of two high technology industrial parks at Chonan and Kwangju and the establishment of central and regional investment promotion offices which also operate as one stop shops to assist foreign investors. The shifting of promotional measures to the Ministry of Trade accords with a strongly held view that has prevailed within the Ministry about the necessity for some government intervention to promote economic activity and foreign investment. The increased level of tax incentives introduced for a significantly expanded list of high tech industries is also a victory for those who believe that more needs to be done to attract investment than leaving it to the general economic environment.

The depth of institutional reform as well as the compromises within the state which have been necessary to effect reform on this single issue does not augur well for rapid policy change in other areas. Attempts at more deregulation by the Kim government have met significant opposition from within the bureaucracy. This impacts on foreign investment policy reform because once inside the country foreign firms are confronted by the more general regulatory environment. The emphasis of the current regime on deregulation has involved the establishment of no fewer than 5 separate committees and the continuation of 2 further committees from the previous government (Kim I.J. 1995: 174–83). However, the work of the Centre for Regulation Studies attached to the FKI's Korea Economic Research Institute has shown the limited success of deregulatory measures to date. Their work suggests that deregulatory measures have only taken place in relation to minor matters while leaving the bigger issue such as the state's control over pricing and entry requirements largely untouched (Kim I.J. 1995: 183–6; Lee S.C. 1995: 158–62).

The reasons for the lack of success have been attributed to an unwillingness of the bureaucracy to give up their power in relation to industry. Deregulation leads to less readily available instruments to control the specific economic activities of business firms and hence less bargaining power for the state. This in turn threatens the position of power which the bureaucracy have long held over economic activity. As stated earlier, it takes a considerable period of time to change the mindset of public officials who have been schooled in an interventionist philosophy particularly when the maintenance of it is in their interests. This also explains why efforts at deregulation have only been partly successful other than in those areas in which the president has taken a personal interest and specific timetables prepared with monitoring mechanisms in place to ensure their implementation.

The key to the reform that has taken place has rested upon Kim's proclaimed belief that the way forward for Korea lies in opening to the outside world and the continuing structural power of the president in the Korean political system to translate such ideas into policy. His keen support for the terms of the new GATT accord, even though it caused significant political difficulties, as well as his support for the APEC initiative and Korea's accession to the OECD all highlight this. The implications are that Kim has strongly supported previous attempts at reducing the government's role where this posed a difficulty in achieving the internationalisation objective. This has been apparent particularly in area of foreign investment.

Conclusion

This chapter has shown that the division within the state which plagued foreign investment policy reform during the Chun and Roh eras is capable of resolution. However, this resolution has required strong leadership, institutional changes, a degree of insulation from societal forces and the appeal to a new ideology in an attempt to carry society along with the state's goals.

The ability of the state to insulate itself from societal pressure on this issue resulted from top policy makers in the state, external actors and big business interests all accepting the need for deregulation. Opposition which might have been encountered from small business and the labour movement did not eventuate because of the lack of institutionalised access for these groups, the continuing structural dominance of the executive over the national assembly and possibly an acceptance of the state's goals of internationalisation.

The institutional changes which have allowed reform to take place not only extended to presidential leadership and the placement of reformers in positions of power but also to institutional changes which allowed different areas of the bureaucracy to take control of different parts of foreign investment policy in ways which matched their long held attitudes to it.

The differing approaches have been at the heart of the issue. Free market advocates have desired a foreign investment policy which removes entry barriers and provides no special incentives so that foreign investment can flow to those sectors that the market dictates. Interventionists argue that more needs to be done to capture the benefits from the preserve of foreign firms. The Kim Young Sam administration has removed restrictions to a considerable extent and placed jurisdiction over this with the Ministry of Finance and Economy which has tended towards a market oriented view. On the other hand it has accepted the need for intervention to ensure that Korea captures the benefits of technology transfer from foreign investment. The administration has placed the technology policy aspect of foreign investment policy with the Ministry of Trade, Industry and Energy which has traditionally held a view that some intervention is necessary.

Conclusion

This book commenced with a discussion of the alternative approaches to foreign investment policy. The market oriented approach was described as favouring a minimalist policy position. Restrictions on foreign investment should not exist because these tend to lead to misallocations of foreign investment flows to sectors which might not necessarily be the most internationally competitive within the economy. At the same time restrictions tend to protect local industries from foreign competition resulting in those sectors of the economy becoming inefficient. Free market advocates also believe that investment incentives are a waste of public resources because investment decisions are made on a range of factors in which incentives figure only marginally.

Interventionists on the other hand believe that there are dangers with a completely free market approach. Foreign investment can lead to whole sectors of an economy being dominated by foreign firms which may in turn result in adverse balance of payments effects which have flow on effects for management of the economy. As well, foreign firms will typically locate in higher value added sectors. In extreme cases this can result in a dual economy where foreign firms and a local elite exist in a modern economy but where the majority of the population lives in relative poverty and pursues low value added activities.

Interventionists believe that policy measures are necessary to avoid industry domination through restrictions on foreign firms in sectors which are of significance to overall industrial development. They also believe that controls are needed to ensure that there is a contribution to the balance of payments through the imposition of conditions such as minimum export levels. In addition, policy measures are necessary to ensure that local firms learn from the technology that foreign firms bring with them. This can occur through joint venture arrangements and controls over technology transfer. In order to implement interventionist policies, it is therefore necessary to have a competent investment agency which screens foreign investment proposals and is able to impose conditions to ensure that benefits do occur.

In the 1960s and 1970s Korean policy makers adopted an interventionist approach to foreign investment. This approach was effective in achieving outcomes which accorded with their objectives. A range of restrictive and incentive measures were used to channel foreign investment into those industries seen by policy makers at the time as priorities for development. These included large industrial infrastructure projects and selected export oriented industries. From 1973, foreign investment policy was made more restrictive by imposing strict criteria for the determination of the contribution that foreign firms could make in terms of technology or international marketing skills.

Policy makers had been prompted to make these changes because they had become aware of some adverse economic consequences from foreign investment in other countries but perhaps more importantly because legitimacy concerns required them to be seen to be taking a much tougher stance. They were able to make the necessary changes to policy relatively easily while at the same time ensuring that the foreign investment which was admitted had continued benefits for Korea. These benefits included the acquisition of technology in industries where technology could not be obtained more cost effectively through licensing or informal methods of acquisition. They also included imparting international marketing skills to Korean firms. After 1973 foreign investment was confined to those export industries where Korean firms had not yet adequately demonstrated an ability to tap international markets. At the same time policy makers were able to achieve a net capital inflow from foreign investment. This was an achievement which was unusual among developing countries of the period as demonstrated by the work of Lall and Streeten (1977).

However, from 1980 key policy makers wished to change policy direction towards a more free market approach. The attempts to do so proved to be ineffective as evidenced by the incremental change that occurred to policy during the 1980s and early 1990s. Policy outcomes also failed to meet the objectives of top policy makers. They had aimed to increase foreign investment flows so that it would assume a much greater proportion of capital inflows. It was also expected to play a greater role in assisting Korean companies acquire technology and in developing competitiveness. Yet by the beginning of the 1990s there was little evidence that it had been able to contribute to these goals. Lower level bureaucrats had continued to pursue restrictive policies in order to protect Korean firms and because they believed that more interventionist strategies were needed to ensure that Korean firms gained from the technology of foreign firms. The success of interventionist policies during the 1960s and 1970s had also led to a certain reluctance to abandon them.

It has only been since 1993 that top policy makers have once again had considerable success in giving effect to their objectives. Significant changes in foreign investment policy have occurred most notably in the removal of entry barriers. While it is still too early to assess the outcomes of these policy changes there are tentative indications that they may be having the desired effect in increasing investment flows. Further research will need to be undertaken in the future to establish the contribution that increased flows of foreign investment have made to the development of the technological capability of Korean firms.

There are several major questions which arise out of this history. The first concerns the ability of the Korean state in the 1960s and 1970s to pursue an interventionist approach. The second aspect requiring explanation is why top policy makers were not able to effectively change direction in the early 1980s. The third is why the current administration has been able to achieve some success in the formulation and implementation of a new foreign investment policy.

An answer to these questions can be found by examining features of the political economy of development. In particular this book has emphasised that effective policy formulation and implementation depends upon state capacity. In turn state capacity needs to be separated into bureaucratic capacity and political capacity. Further bureaucratic capacity and political capacity each have various elements which need to be disaggregated in order to understand why each is important in policy processes. Finally, bureaucratic capacity and political capacity reinforce each other in determining state capacity in relation to any particular issue.

The elements of bureaucratic capacity which have been emphasised include the structuring of institutions, leadership and ideology and how these combined in relation to the issue of foreign investment. The first of these was the structuring of the bureaucratic institutions of the state. In the Korean developmental state jurisdiction over foreign investment lay with the Economic Planning Board. Its structural position within the bureaucracy, its close ties to the presidential office and its ability to permeate other key parts of the economic bureaucracy considerably assisted policy cohesiveness. When control over foreign investment policy was moved to the Ministry of Finance in the early 1980s, cohesiveness suffered because of the inability of this ministry to exercise the same coordinating role as had been played by the Economic Planning Board. As a result the Ministry of Finance was unable to resolve conflicts which arose between it and other ministries and between other ministries themselves concerning the benefits of particular investment projects or concerning the extent to which policy should be changed.

The essential reason for the differences of opinion revolved around the extent to which Korean industries should continue to be protected from foreign competition. Top policy makers in the Ministry of Finance and the Economic Planning Board had accepted the need for a more liberal approach whereas significant elements within other ministries were concerned about the effects of such an approach on local industry and on their own positions of power.

The conflicting views within the bureaucracy have only been able to be resolved by deregulation which has considerably reduced the role of the bureaucracy in relation to foreign investment and by brokering a compromise between competing views concerning the role of the state. The devolution of the promotional aspects of foreign investment policy to the Ministry of Trade and Industry has accorded with the traditional views held by this ministry that more needs to be done than leaving foreign investment to market forces. Similarly, the views of the Ministry of Finance that a free market approach should be adopted have been met by simplification of the approval process and the planned removal of specific barriers to foreign investment in most industries.

Leadership has also been seen to be an integral element in ensuring the policy cohesiveness that bureaucratic capacity implies. This accords with the views of others such as Liddell (1992) and Gourevitch (1993) who make the point that leadership does matter and can be a significant determinant of policy outcomes. In the Korean developmental state, Park's single minded pursuit of economic growth, his willingness to sanction and support a large degree of state intervention to bring this about and personal attention to the details of economic policy assisted considerably in the development of foreign investment policies which would harness foreign investors in the pursuit of the developmental goals of the state. At the same time, Park paid attention to the issue of loyalty within the bureaucracy and to implementation of policy by not only ensuring a military influence in key positions but by structuring the bureaucracy along the lines of the successful military-like Japanese model which had influenced him.

The role of leadership and the constraints upon it is further illustrated in the Chun and Roh eras. In each case, the president faced constraints in playing a significant role in economic policy matters. In Chun's case, the initial state of the economy when he came to office, the need to secure legitimacy and the presence of competing ideas within his administration as to how legitimacy might be enhanced, as well as a lack of detailed knowledge of economic matters, saw him delegate much of the details of economic policy to others. In Roh's case, preoccupation with international affairs and a belief in leaving economic policy matters to the various ministers as well as legitimacy concerns and the downsizing of his personal presidential staff meant less direct involvement in economic policy matters. This deprived key areas of economic policy making of the personal attention of top political leaders and made the resolution of conflicts more difficult. Foreign investment policy change was one area that suffered as a result.

By way of contrast, Kim Young Sam has been motivated to take a keen personal interest in foreign investment policy. This has been due to a personal goal of internationalising the Korean economy. The Kim government has been a keen participant in international economic institutions including APEC, the new WTO, and the Asia-Europe Economic Forum. In addition Korea's joining the OECD has propelled the administration to take steps to bring its regulations into line with other members. All of these factors have led to Kim taking a keen interest in liberalisation on those issues which directly affect his internationalisation policy. Foreign investment has been one of those issues.

As well as institutional arrangements and leadership, a key determinant of bureaucratic capacity is the value system which holds the bureaucracy together. It has been argued throughout this book that ideology has been fundamental to the maintenance of cohesiveness within the Korean state. During the Park era, the bureaucracy was strengthened by the widespread acceptance of Park's developmental ideology. Bureaucrats were motivated by it not only because of its promise to improve their living standards but because it reinforced their own positions of influence. When top policy makers at the beginning of the Chun regime expressed the desire to move to a more market oriented position, the deregulation and consequent loss of power that this implied was strongly resisted. This occurred not only because bureaucrats perceived that old policies had worked well and because their own positions were under threat but also because they had been schooled in an interventionist approach. In addition, a certain lack of respect which the bureaucracy held for the Chun regime only strengthened their resolve to oppose the reforms proposed. The divide between market oriented and interventionist objectives for economic policy continued during the Roh era. The lack of leadership reinforced the growing divide within the state and prevented the resolution of conflicts over economic policy direction.

The Kim government has only been able to resolve these differences of opinion within the bureaucracy to a limited degree as research by the Centre for Regulation Studies has made clear. The involvement of the leadership has been able to carry the bureaucracy along to a considerable degree with the policy reforms on specific issues that affect internationalisation, such as foreign investment. However, in other areas deregulation has run up against the opposition of bureaucrats not only because it affects their personal positions of power but because of the entrenched belief within the bureaucracy in a more interventionist style of economic management.

Bureaucratic capacity is a necessary but insufficient condition for achieving policy outcomes that accord with objectives. In order for policies to achieve their objectives, policy makers must be able to carry society along with policy goals. For this reason a number of authors have suggested that, in addition to bureaucratic capacity, it is political capacity which is determinative of policy outcomes.

The examination of the state's political capacity in this book drew attention to the need to analyse separately the state's relationship to major societal groups such as business and labour. It also drew attention to the need to examine political capacity in terms of the relationship between the executive branch of government and the legislative branch which is the formal representative body for the expression of societal concerns. Political capacity requires the state to maintain a degree of insulation from societal pressures in its policy making while at the same time maintaining sufficient embeddedness to ensure acceptance and therefore effective implementation of policies.

This work has argued that in the Korean developmental state of the 1960s and 1970s, the state's political capacity arose partly as a result of its formation of a development coalition with big business interests in which the state was the dominant partner. At the same time, the formal institutions of the state were structured in such a way as to exclude indirect societal input into policy matters via the national assembly. Other societal groups, such as the labour movement, were also effectively excluded from input by corporatist arrangements and by the enforcement of unpopular policy measures through the coercive agencies of the state.

The effectiveness of the state's foreign investment policy in achieving the objectives of top policy makers was due in part to the close ties which the state had with big business groups. This allowed the state to consult with business not only in the formation of policies but also in decisions regarding particular investment projects. On the other hand, while the state excluded other societal actors from a formal input into policy in this area, opposition to foreign investment that came from the national assembly and informal opposition groups brought forth a response from the state in the interests of maintaining legitimacy. The tightening up of foreign investment policy in the early 1970s was as much a result of the informal opposition to it as it was a response to the possible adverse economic consequences which unfettered flows of foreign investment can have in a developing country.

It has been argued that in the Chun era the state was able to maintain its insulation on this issue to a considerable extent due to the continuation of a similar pattern of relationships with societal groups as had prevailed in the Park era. Despite a split developing in the development coalition on major issues such as restructuring as a result of the over capacity that had resulted from the heavy and chemical industry policies and the phasing out of declining industries, foreign investment policy matters remained largely unaffected. In the case of other societal groups, repression by the state prevented any formal or informal input into most areas of policy. However informal groups were active in building general opposition to the repressive regime which was finally overthrown in a people power revolution in June 1987.

In the newly democratised environment that characterised the period that Roh Tae Woo was in office, societal groups gained an ability to pursue their interests much more directly. The national assembly came to be dominated by opposition parties in the 1988–90 period, the labour movement successfully achieved a long overdue improvement in wages and conditions and business groups became much more vocal in demanding that the state withdraw from intervention in their affairs. The cross cutting pressures that societal groups posed for the Roh government are well illustrated by the case of foreign investment policy. Labour and informal opposition groups pushed for continued controls over foreign investment in the interests of their own members. The opposition and even the government party in the national assembly pressured the Roh administration not to deregulate too quickly because of the implication this would have for their business constituents and hence their own positions.

Business groups on the other hand wanted to be freed from the controls that the state held over their economic activity but at the same time wanted the maintenance of continuing subsidy measures. This sent conflicting signals to the state on foreign investment policy which consisted of both restrictive and incentive measures. The patrimonial ties between business groups and the government which had existed from the days of the Park regime continued under Roh which made it difficult for him to deregulate. To deregulate would have deprived his administration of the particularistic advantages which could be handed out in exchange for political funding and therefore led to a lack of motivation to implement deregulation policies.

The Roh era also saw the beginning of the state's inability to insulate itself from international pressure on the foreign investment policy issue. During the Park and Chun administrations, Korea's major trading partner and political ally, the United States, had allowed the Korean government to have a protectionist policy because of the significance of Korea in the western anti soviet alliance system. However as from the mid 1980s, the United States began to pressure the Korean government for increased access to the Korean market. With the end of the cold war and the increasing importance of international economic issues on the international agenda, this pressure was increased.

The Roh regime therefore faced conflicting internal pressures concerning foreign investment policy change as well as external pressure. In the newly democratised environment, these conflicting societal pressures made it difficult for the administration to undertake radical reform. The conflicting societal pressures and the increased ability of societal groups to permeate the state exacerbated the ideological divide that existed between top policy makers and working level bureaucrats. Thus the diminution in political capacity reinforced the reduced bureaucratic capacity for policy change.

Kim has consistently emphasised the goal of internationalisation of the Korean economy demonstrating an attempt to motivate and unify societal forces and the bureaucracy through an appeal to ideology. Kim's success in achieving policy objectives in relation to foreign investment stem from the reinforcement of this goal by strong leadership, institutional reform and from the control that he has been able to exercise over the national assembly. At the same time he has faced little opposition from big business on deregulation of foreign investment controls. Any opposition from smaller firms the labour movement and other societal groups has been able to be minimised by the combination of some acceptance of the new ideology of internationalisation and at the same time the lack of any form of institutionalised access for these societal groups to the policy making processes of the state.

This book has argued that an understanding of policy change and effectiveness can be gained from an appreciation of bureaucratic capacity and political capacity and how the two work together in determining the state's overall capacity in relation to any particular issue. An analysis of the various elements of bureaucratic and political capacity provides a useful explanation of the chequered history of foreign investment policy and its outcomes in Korea over the past three decades.

Bibliography

Adams, F.G. and Davis, I.M. 1994, 'The role of policy in economic development: comparisons of the East Asian and Latin American experience', *Asian Pacific Economic Literature*, vol. 8, no. 1, pp. 8–26.

Agodo, O. 1978, 'The determinants of U.S. private manufacturing investments in Africa', *Journal of International Business Studies*, Winter, pp. 95–107.

Ahiakpor, J.C. 1990, *Multinationals and Economic Development: An Integration of Competing Theories*, Routledge, London.

Ahn, B.S., Kil, S.H. and Kim, K.W. 1988, *Elections in Korea*, Seoul Computer Press, Seoul.

American Chamber of Commerce in Korea 1994, *Trade and Investment Issues: U.S. and Korea*, Seoul.

Amirahmadi, H. 1989, 'Development paradigms at a crossroad and the South Korean experience', *Journal of Contemporary Asia*, vol. 19, no. 2, pp. 167–85.

Amsden, A.H. 1989, *Asia's Next Giant: South Korea and Late Industrialization*, Oxford University Press, New York.

Amsden, A.H. 1994a, 'The specter of Anglo Saxonization is haunting South Korea', in *Korea's Political Economy: An Institutional Perspective*, eds L.J. Cho and Y.H. Kim, Westview Press, Boulder, Colorado.

Amsden, A.H. 1994b, 'Why isn't the whole world experimenting with the East Asian model to develop?: a review of "The East Asian Miracle"', *World Development*, vol. 22, no. 4, pp. 627–33.

Amsden, A.H. and Euh, Y.D. 1993, 'South Korea's 1980s financial reforms: good-bye financial repression (maybe), hello new institutional restraints', *World Development*, vol. 21, no. 3, pp. 379–90.

Amsden, A.H. and Kim, Linsu 1986, 'Technological perspective on the general machinery industry in the Republic of Korea', in *Machinery and Economic Development*, ed. M. Fransman, Macmillan, London.

Aranda, V. 1988, 'National policies on FDI in the 1980s', *The CTC Reporter*, no. 26, pp. 34–7.

Argheyd, K. and Seguin-Dulude, L. 1991, 'Investment climate in East Asia', *Business Quarterly*, Autumn, pp. 47–52.

Bae, J.T. and Lee, J.J. 1986, 'Technology development patterns of small and medium sized companies in the Korean machinery industry', *Technovation*, vol. 4, pp. 279–96.

Balassa, B. 1991, *Economic Policies in the Pacific Area Developing Countries*, Macmillan, London.

Bark, D.S. and Lee, C.J. 1976, 'Bureaucratic elite and development orientation', in *Political Leadership in Korea*, eds D.S. Suh and C.J. Lee, University of Washington Press, Seattle.

Bartlett, B. 1984, 'Trade policy and the dangers of protectionism', in *The Industrial Policy Debate*, ed. C. Johnson, I.C.S. Press, San Francisco.

Behrman, J.N. and Grosse, R.E. 1990, *International Business and Governments: Issues and Institutions*, University of South Carolina Press, Columbia, South Carolina.

Bhagwati, J. 1966, *The Economics of Underdeveloped Countries*, Weidenfeld and Nicolson, London.

Biggs, T.S. and Levy, B.D. 1991, 'Strategic interventions and the political economy of industrial policy in developing countries', in *Reforming Economic Systems in Developing Countries*, eds D.S. Perkins and M. Roemer, Harvard University Press, Cambridge, Mass.

Billet, B.L. 1991, *Investment Behaviour of Multinational Corporations in Developing Areas*, Transaction Publishers, New Brunswick, New Jersey.

Boadway, R. and Shah, A. 1992, *How Tax Incentives Affect Decisions to Invest in Developing Countries,* Policy Research Public Economics Working Paper 1011, The World Bank, Washington.

Bradshaw, Y.W., Kim, Y.I. and London, B. 1993, 'Transnational economic linkages, the state and dependent development in South Korea 1966–1988: a time series analysis', *Social Forces*, vol. 72, no. 2, pp. 315–45.

Byington, L. 1990, 'The effects of the Korean labour movement on the economy of the Republic of Korea and on U.S. investment in the Republic of Korea', *Journal of International Law and Economics*, vol. 24, pp. 149–93.

Byun, H.Y. and Wang, Y.J. 1994, *Technology Transfer and Multinational Corporations: The Case of South Korea*, Korea Institute for International Economic Policy, Seoul.

Caiden, G. and Jung, Y.D. 1985, 'The political economy of Korean development under the Park government', in *Administrative Dynamics and Development: The Korean Experience*, eds B.W. Kim, D.S. Bell and C.B. Lee, Kyobo Publishing Co., Seoul.

Castells, M. 1992, 'Four Asian tigers with a dragon head: a comparative analysis of the state, economy, and society in the Asian Pacific rim', in *States and Development in the Asian Pacific Rim*, eds R.P. Applebaum and J. Henderson, Sage Publications, London.

Chan, S. and Clark, C. 1995, 'Do MNCs matter for national development? contrasting East Asia and Latin America', in *FDI in a Changing Global Political Economy*, eds C. Clark and S. Chan, Macmillan, London.

Chang, H.J. 1993, 'The political economy of industrial policy in Korea', *Cambridge Journal of Economics*, vol. 17, pp. 131–57.

Chang, H.J. and Kozul-Wright, R. 1994, 'Organising development: comparing national systems of entrepreneurship in Sweden and South Korea', *The Journal of Development Studies*, vol. 30, no. 3, pp. 859–81.

Chase Dunn, C. 1987, 'The Korean trajectory in the world system', in *Dependency Issues in Korean Development,* ed. K.D. Kim, Seoul National University Press, Seoul.

Cho, L.J. and Kim, Y.H. 1994, 'A new vision for institutional reform', in *Korea's Political Economy: An Institutional Perspective*, eds L.J. Cho and Y.D. Euh, Westview Press, Boulder, Colorado.

Cho, S.C. 1975, 'The bureaucracy', in *Korean Politics in Transitions*, ed. E.R. Wright, University of Washington Press, Seattle.

Cho, Soon 1994, *The Dynamics of Korean Economic Development*, Institute for International Economics, Washington.

Choi, B.S. 1991a, *Economic Policy Making in Korea: Institutional Analysis of Economic Policy Change in the 1970s and 1980s*, Chomyung Press, Seoul.

Choi, B.S. 1991b, 'The structure of the economic policy making institutions in Korea and the strategic role of the EPB', in *A Dragon's Progress: Development Administration in Korea*, eds G.E. Caiden and B.W. Kim, Kumarian Press, Connecticut.

Choi, B.S. 1993, 'The changing conception of industrial policymaking in Korea', in *Korean Public Administration and Policy in Transition: Vol 2 Substantive Public Policies*, eds K.W. Kim and Y.D. Jung, Jangwon Publishing Co., Seoul.

Choi, J.J. 1989, *Labour and the Authoritarian State: Labor Unions in South Korean Manufacturing Industries, 1961–1980*, Korea University Press, Seoul.

Choi, J.W. 1993, 'Policy making process in Korea: the enactment process of the monopoly regulation and fair trade act', in *Korean Public Administration and Policy in Transition: Vol 2 Substantive Public Policies*, eds K.W. Kim and Y.D. Jung, Jangwon Publishing Co., Seoul.

Choi, Y.H. and Lee, Y.H. 1995, 'Political reform and the government-business (Chaebol) relationship in South Korea', *Korea Observer*, vol. 27, 100th Special Issue, pp. 39–61.

Chu, K.I. 1989, The role of the foreign capital inducement law for the development of the Korean economy: foreign investment considerations, paper presented to the Lawasia Conference, Hong Kong, September 1989.

Chung, B.S. and Lee, C.H. 1980, *The Choice of Production Techniques by Foreign and Local Firms in Korea*, The University of Chicago Press, Chicago.

Chung, C.K. 1985, 'Policy making in the executive branch: application of an American model to three Korean case studies', in *Administrative Dynamics and Development: The Korean Experience*, eds B.W Kim, D.S. Bell and C.B. Lee, Kyobo Publishing Co., Seoul.

Chung, C.K. 1986, 'The ideology of economic development and its impact on policy process', *The Korean Journal of Policy Studies*, vol. 1, pp. 28–46.

Chung, C.K. 1989, 'Presidential decision making and bureaucratic expertise in Korea', *Governance: An International Journal of Policy and Administration*, vol. 2, no. 3, pp. 267–92.

Chung, C.K. 1995, *Economic Leadership of the Presidents: Economic Policy Management Under the Governments of Park Chong-Hee, Chon Tu-Hwan, Roh Te-Wu*, Seoul National University Press, Seoul.

Chung, C.K. and Jun, J.S. 1993, 'The irony of cutback reform: the Korean experience during a period of turbulent transition', in *Korean Public Administration and Policy in Transition: Vol. 1 Governmental Institutions and Policy Process*, eds K.W. Kim and Y.D. Jung, Jangwon Publishing Co., Seoul.

Chung, J.Y. 1995, 'The Uruguary round negotiation: process, result, and beyond', in *Korea's Economic Diplomacy: Survival as a Trading Nation*, The Sejong Institute, Seoul.

Clark, C. and Chan, S. 1994, 'The developmental roles of the state: moving beyond the developmental state in conceptualizing Asian political economies', *Governance: An International Journal of Policy and Administration*, vol. 7, no. 4, pp. 332–59.

Clark, C. and Chan, S. (eds) 1995, *FDI in a Changing Global Political Economy*, Macmillan, London.

Clifford, M. 1994, *Business, Bureaucrats and Generals in South Korea*, Armonk, New York.

Cohen, B. 1975, *Multinational Firms and Asian Exports*, Yale University Press, New Haven.

Contractor, F.J. 1990, 'Ownership patterns of U.S. joint ventures abroad and the liberalization of foreign government regulations in the 1980s: evidence from the benchmark surveys', *Journal of International Business Studies*, First Quarter, pp. 55–73.

Corbo, V. and Suh, S.M. 1992, *Structural Adjustment in a Newly Industrialised Country: The Korean Experience*, John Hopkins University Press, Baltimore.

Cotton, J. 1989, 'From authoritarianism to democracy in South Korea', *Political Studies*, vol. 37, pp. 244–59.

Cotton, J. 1991, 'The limits to liberalisation in industrializing Asia: three views of the State', *Pacific Affairs*, vol. 64, no. 3, pp. 311–27.

Cotton, J. 1994, 'The state in the Asian NICS', *Asian Perspective*, vol. 18, no. 1, pp. 39–56.

Cumings, B. 1987, 'The origins and development of the Northeast Asian political economy: industrial sectors, product cycles and political consequences', in *The Political Economy of the New Asian Industrialisation*, ed. F. Deyo, Cornell University Press, Ithaca.

Cumings, B. 1991, 'The legacy of Japanese colonialism in Korea', in *The Japanese Colonial Empire, 1895–1945*, eds R.H. Myers and M.R. Peattie, Princeton University Press, Princeton, New. Jersey.

Dalton, B. 1993, 'Economic liberalisation in the Republic of Korea', *Asian Studies Review*, vol. 17, no. 2, pp. 63–79.

Deyo, F.C. 1987, 'State and labour: modes of political exclusion in East Asian development', in *The Political Economy of the New Asian Industrialism*, ed. F.C. Deyo, Cornell University Press, Ithaca.

Deyo, F.C. 1989a, *Beneath the Miracle: Labour Subordination in the New Asian Industrialisation*, University of California Press, Berkeley.

Deyo, F.C. 1989b, 'Labour and development policy in East Asia', *The Annals of the American Academy of Political and Social Science*, vol. 505, pp. 152–61.

Deyo, F.C., Haggard, S. and Koo, H. 1987, 'Labour in the political economy of East Asian industrialization', *Bulletin of Concerned Asian Scholars*, vol. 19, no. 2, pp. 42–53.

Doner, R.F. 1992, 'Limits of state strength: toward an institutionalist view of economic development', *World Politics*, vol. 44, pp. 398–431.

Dunning, J.H. 1986, *Japanese Participation in British Industry*, Croom Helm, London.

Dunning, J.H. 1988, *Explaining International Production*, Unwin: Hyman, London.

Dunning, J.H. and Narula, R. 1994, 'Transpacific foreign direct investment and the investment development path: the record assessed', in *Essays in International Business*, Centre for International Business Education and Research, The University of South Carolina.

Eckert, C. 1993, 'The South Korean bourgeoisie: a class in search of hegemony, in *State and Society in Contemporary Korea*, ed. H. Koo, Cornell University Press, Ithaca.

Encarnation, D.J. 1989, *Dislodging Multinationals: India's Strategy in Comparative Perspective*, Cornell University Press, Ithaca.

Encarnation, D.J. and Wells, L.T. 1985, 'Sovereignty en garde: negotiating with foreign investors', *International Organisation*, vol. 39, no. 1, pp. 185–216.

Enos, J.L. 1984, 'Government intervention in the transfer of technology: the case of South Korea', *IDS Bulletin*, vol. 15, no. 2, pp. 26–31.

Enos, J.L. 1989, 'Transfer of technology', *Asian-Pacific Economic Literature*, vol. 3, no. 1, pp. 3–37.

European Community Chamber of Commerce in Korea 1994, *Trade Issues 1994*, Seoul.

Evans, P.B. 1979, *Dependent Development: The Alliance of Multinational, State and Local Capital in Brazil*, Princeton University Press, Princeton, New Jersey.

Evans, P.B. 1985, 'Transnational linkages and the economic role of the state: an analysis of developing and industrialised nations in the post World War 11 period', in *Bringing the State Back In,* eds P. B. Evans, D. Rueschemeyer and T. Skocpol, Cambridge University Press, Cambridge.

Evans, P.B. 1987a, 'Dependency and the state in recent Korean development: some comparisons with Latin American NICs', in *Dependency Issues in Korean Development*, ed. K.D. Kim, Seoul National University Press, Seoul.

Evans, P.B. 1987b, 'Class, state and dependence in East Asia: lessons for Latin Americanists', in *The Political Economy of the New Asian Industrialism*, ed. F. Deyo, Cornell University Press, Ithaca.

Evans, P.B. 1992, 'The state as problem and solution: predation, embedded autonomy, and structural change', in *The Politics of Economic Adjustment: International Constraints, Distributive Politics and the State*, eds S. Haggard and R. Kaufman, Princeton University Press, Princeton, New Jersey.

Evans, P.B. 1995, *Embedded Autonomy: States and Industrial Transformation*, Princeton University Press, Princeton, New Jersey.

Evans, P.B., Rueschemeyer, D. and Skocpol, T.(eds) 1985, *Bringing the State Back In*, Cambridge University Press, Cambridge.

Foster Carter, A. 1987, 'Standing up: the two Korean states and the dependency debate—a bipartisan approach', in *Dependency Issues in Korean Development*, ed. K.D. Kim, Seoul National University Press, Seoul.

Fry, M.J. 1993a, *Foreign Debt Investment in Southeast Asia—Differential Impacts*, Institute of Southeast Asian Studies, Singapore.

Fry, M.J. 1993b, *Foreign Direct Investment in a Macroeconomic Framework: Finance Efficiency Incentives and Distortions*, Policy Research Debt and International Finance Working Paper 1141, World Bank, Washington.

Fry, M.J. 1995, 'Financial development in Asia: some analytical issues', *Asian-Pacific Economic Literature*, vol. 9, no. 1, pp. 40–57.

Gereffi, G. 1992, 'New realities of industrial development in East Asia and Latin America: global regional and national trends', in *States and Development in the Asian Pacific Rim*, eds R.P. Applebaum and J. Henderson, Sage Publications, London.

Gerschenkron, A. 1952, 'Economic backwardness in historical perspective', in *The Progress of Underdeveloped Areas*, ed. B.F. Hoselitz, Harvard University Press, Cambridge, Mass.

Gibney, F. 1992, *Korea's Quiet Revolution: From Garrison State To Democracy*, Walter and Co., New York.

Globerman, S. 1988, 'Government policies toward foreign direct investment: has a new era dawned?', *Columbia Journal of World Business*, vol. 23, no. 3, pp. 41–9.

Gold, D. 1991, 'The determinants of FDI and their implications for host developing countries', *The CTC Reporter*, no. 31, pp. 21–4.

Goldsborough, D. 1985, 'Foreign direct investment in developing countries', *Finance and Development*, March, pp. 31–4.

Goldsmith, A.A. 1995, 'The state, the market and economic development: a second look at Adam Smith in theory and practice', *Development and Change*, vol. 26, no. 4, pp. 633–50.

Gourevitch, P.A. 1993, 'Democracy and economic policy: elective affinities and circumstantial conjectures', *World Development*, vol. 21, no. 8, pp. 1271–80.

Grieco, J.M. 1986, 'Foreign investment and development: theories and evidence', in *Investing In Development: New Roles for Private Capital*, eds T. H. Moran and others, Transaction Books, New Brunswick.

Guisinger, S.E. and Associates 1985, *Investment Incentives and Performance Requirements—Patterns of International Trade, Production and Investment*, Praeger Publishers, New York.

Guisinger, S.E. 1986, 'Host country policies to attract and control foreign investment', in *Investing In Development: New Roles for Private Capital*, eds T. H. Moran and others, Transaction Books, New Brunswick.

Ha, T.K. 1993, 'Selection patterns of the Korean senior civil service', in *Korean Public Administration And Policy in Transition: Vol 1 Governmental Institutions and Policy Process*, eds K.W. Kim and Y.D. Jung, Jangwon Publishing Co., Seoul.

Ha, Y.S. 1993, 'State intervention, fiscal policy and industrialization in Korea', in *Korean Public Administration and Policy in Transition; Vol 2 Substantive Public Policies*, eds K.W. Kim and Y.D. Jung, Jangwon Publishing Co., Seoul.

Haggard, S. 1988, 'The politics of industrialisation in the Republic of Korea and Taiwan', in *Achieving Industrialisation in East Asia*, ed. H. Hughes, Cambridge University Press, Cambridge.

Haggard, S. 1990, *Pathways from the Periphery: The Politics of Growth in Newly Industrializing Countries*, Cornell University Press, Ithaca.

Haggard, S. 1994, 'Business, politics and policy in Northeast and Southeast Asia', in *Business and Government in Industrialising Asia*, ed. A. MacIntyre, Allen and Unwin, Sydney.

Haggard, S. and Cheng, T. 1987, 'State and foreign capital in the East Asian NICs', in *The Political Economy of the New Asian Industrialism*, ed. F. Deyo, Cornell University Press, Ithaca.

Haggard, S. and Moon, C.I. 1990, 'Institutions and economic policy: theory and a Korean case study', *World Politics*, vol. 42, no. 2 (January), pp. 210–37.

Han, S.J. 1987, 'Political institutionalization in South Korea, 1961–1984', in *Asian Political Institutionalization*, eds R. Scalapino, S. Sato and J Wandeli, Institute of East Asian Studies, University of California, Berkeley.

Harris, N. 1992, 'States, economic development, and the Asian Pacific rim', in *States and Development in the Asian Pacific Rim*, eds R.P. Applebaum and J. Henderson, Sage Publications, London.

Healey, D. and Lutkenhorst, W. 1989, 'Export processing zones: the case of the Republic of Korea', *Industry and Development*, vol. 26, pp. 1–36.

Helleiner, G.K. 1991, 'Direct foreign investment and manufacturing for export: a review of the issues', in *Foreign Direct Investments*, eds H.W. Singer, N. Hatti and R. Tandon, Indus Publishing Company, New Delhi.

Hill, H. and Johns, B. 1991, 'The role of direct foreign investment in developing East Asian countries' in *Foreign Direct Investments*, eds H.W. Singer, N. Hatti and R. Tandon, Indus Publishing Company, New Delhi.

Hinton, H.C. 1983, *Korea Under New Leadership: The Fifth Republic*, Praeger, New York.

Hirschman, A.O. 1958, *The Strategy of Economic Development*, Yale University Press, New Haven, Connecticut.

Holder, M. 1987, 'Industrial co-operation and small and medium industries: the Korean-French experience', in *Dependency Issues in Korean Development*, ed. K.D. Kim, Seoul National University Press, Seoul.

Hong, Y.S. 1994, *Technology Transfer: The Korean Experience*, Korean Institute for International Economic Policy Working Paper No. 94–03, Seoul.

Hymer, S.H. 1979a, 'Direct foreign investment and the national economic interest', in *The Multinational Corporation: A Radical Approach*, eds R.B. Cohen, N. Felton, M. Nkosi and J. van Lierre, Cambridge University Press, Cambridge.

Hymer, S. H. 1979b, 'The internationalization of capital', in *The Multinational Corporation: A Radical Approach*, eds R.B. Cohen, N. Felton, M. Nkosi and J. van Lierre, Cambridge University Press, Cambridge.

Hymer, S.H. 1979c, 'The multinational corporation and the law of uneven development', in *The Multinational Corporation: A Radical Approach*, eds R.B. Cohen, N. Felton, M. Nkosi and J. van Lierre, Cambridge University Press, Cambridge.

Hymer, S.H. and Rowthorn, R. 1979, 'Multinational corporations and international oligopoly: the non American challenge' in *The Multinational Corporation: A Radical Approach*, eds R.B. Cohen, N. Felton, M. Nkosi and J. van Lierre, Cambridge University Press, Cambridge.

Im, H.B. 1987, 'The rise of bureaucratic authoritarianism in South Korea', *World Politics*, vol. 39, no. 2, pp. 231–57.

IMF 1985, *Foreign Private Investment in Developing Countries*, IMF Occasional Paper 33, Washington.

Islam, I. 1992, 'Political economy and East Asian economic development', *Asian-Pacific Economic Literature*, vol. 6, no. 2, pp. 69–101.

Islam, I. 1994, 'Between the state and the market: the case for eclectic neoclassical political economy', in *Business and Government in Industrialising Asia*, ed. A. MacIntrye, Allen and Unwin, Sydney.

Islam, I. and Chowdhury, A. (eds) 1993, *The Newly Industrialising Economies of East Asia*, Routledge, London.

Janelli, R.L. 1993, *Making Capitalism: The Social and Cultural Construction of a South Korean Conglomerate*, Stanford University Press, Stanford, California.

Jeon, J.G. 1994, 'The political economy of crisis management in the third world: a comparative study of South Korea and Taiwan (1970s), in *Pacific Affairs*, vol. 67, Winter 94/95, pp. 565–85.

Jo, S.H. 1977, *Direct Foreign Private Investment in South Korea: An Economic Survey*, Korea Modernization Studies Series (4), Korea Development Institute Working Paper 7707, Seoul.

Johnson, C. 1987, 'Political institutions and economic performance: the government-business relationship in Japan, South Korea and Taiwan', in *The Political Economy of the New Asian Industrialism*, ed. F. C. Deyo, Cornell University Press, Ithaca.

Johnson, C. 1989, 'South Korean democratization: the role of economic development', *The Pacific Review*, vol. 2, no. 1, pp. 1–10.

Johnson, C. 1992, Capitalism: East Asian style, paper prepared for the Panglaykim Memorial Lecture, Jakarta, 15 December.

Johnson, C. 1994, 'What is the best system of national economic management for Korea', in *Korea's Political Economy: An Institutional Perspective*, eds L.J. Cho and Y.H. Kim, Westview Press, Boulder, Colorado.

Johnson, H.G. 1967, *Economic Policies Toward Less Developed Countries*, The Brookings Institution, Washington, D.C.

Jones, L.P. 1994, 'Big business groups in South Korea: causation, growth and policies', in *Korea's Political Economy: An Institutional Perspective*, eds L.J. Cho and Y.H. Kim, Westview Press, Boulder, Colorado.

Jones, L.P. and Sakong, I. 1980, 'Government, Business and Entrepreneurship in Economic Development: The Korean Case', *Studies in the Modernization of Korea, 1945–75*, Harvard University Press, Cambridge, Massachusetts.

Jun, J.S. 1985, 'The paradoxes of development: problems of Korea's transformation', in *Administrative Dynamics and Development: The Korean Experience*, eds B.W. Kim, D.S. Bell and C.B. Lee, Kyobo Publishing Co., Seoul.

Jung, K.H. 1988, 'Business-government relations in the growth of Korean business groups', *Korean Social Science Journal*, vol. 14, pp. 69–82.

Jung, S.K. 1991, 'Korean democracy and the limits of political engineering', in *A Dragon's Progress: Development Administration in Korea*, eds G.E. Caiden and B.W. Kim, Kumarian Press, Connecticut.

Jwa, S.H. 1995, *Korea's Recent Capital Flows: Trends, Determinants, and Evaluation*, Korea Development Institute Working Paper No. 9502, Seoul.

Katzenstein, P.J. 1978, *Between Power and Plenty: Foreign Economic Policies of Advanced Industrial States*, University of Wisconsin Press, Madison, Wisconsin.

Katzenstein, P.J. and Tsujinaka, Y. 1995, '"Bullying", "buying", and "binding": U.S.-Japanese transnational relations and domestic structures', in *Bringing Transnational Relations Back In: Non State Actors, Domestic Structures and International Institutions*, ed. T. Risse-Kappen, Cambridge University Press, New York.

Kim, B.K. 1992, 'Economic policy and the Economic Planning Board (EPB) in Korea', *Asian Affairs*, vol. 18, no. 4, pp. 197–213.

Kim, B.K. 1995, *Politics of Democratic Consolidation in Korea: Modernization of Confucianism*, Korea University, Seoul.

Kim, B.W. 1991a, 'An assessment of government intervention in Korean development', in *A Dragon's Progress: Development Administration in Korea*, eds G.E. Caiden and B.W. Kim, Kumarian Press, Connecticut.

Kim, B.W. 1991b, 'Democratization and administrative reform in Korea: a new direction', in *A Dragon's Progress: Development Administration in Korea*, eds G.E. Caiden and B.W. Kim, Kumarian Press, Connecticut.

Kim, B.W. 1993, 'The democratization of public administration in Korea', in *Korean Public Administration and Policy in Transition: Vol. 1 Governmental Institutions and Policy Process*, eds K.W. Kim and Y.D. Jung, Jangwon Publishing Co., Seoul.

Kim, B.W. and Bell, D.S. 1985, 'Bureaucratic elitism and democratic development in Korea', in *Administrative Dynamics and Development: The Korean Experience*, eds B.W. Kim, D.S. Bell and C.B. Lee, Kyobo Publishing Inc., Seoul.

Kim, C.J. (ed) 1988, *Business Laws of Korea*, Pannum Books, Seoul.

Kim, C.L. and Pai, S.T. 1981, *Legislative Process in Korea*, Seoul National University Press, Seoul.

Kim, D.H. 1993, 'The development of indigenous science and technology capabilities in Korea', in *Korean Public Administration and Policy in Transition: Vol. 2 Substantive Public Policies*, eds K.W. Kim and Y.D. Jung, Jangwon Publishing Co., Seoul.

Kim, E.M. 1988, 'From dominance to symbiosis: state and chaebol in Korea', *Pacific Focus*, vol. 3, no. 2, pp. 105–21.

Kim, E.M. 1992, 'The investments of U.S. and Japanese multinational corporations in Korea: a comparative investigation', *Asian Affairs*, pp. 214–27.

Kim, E.M. 1993, 'Contradictions and limits of a developmental state: with illustrations from the South Korean case', *Social Problems*, vol. 40, no. 2, pp. 228–49.

Kim, H. 1993, 'International technology licensing in Korea: policy trends and effects', in *Korean Public Administration and Policy in Transition: Vol. 2 Substantive Public Policies*, eds K.W. Kim and Y.D. Jung, Jangwon Publishing Co., Seoul.

Kim, I.H. 1987, 'Direct foreign investment in Korea', *Korea Exchange Bank Monthly Review*, vol. 21, pp. 3–13.

Kim, I.J. 1995, 'The results and future course of Korea's deregulation policy', in *The Role of the Three Branches of Government for the Rule of Law and the Free Market in Korea*, ed. I.J. Kim, Korea Economic Research Institute, Seoul.

Kim, K.D. and Lee, O.J. 1987, 'Educational background of the Korean elite: the influence of the United States and Japan', in *Dependency Issues in Korean Development,* ed. K.D. Kim, Seoul National University Press, Seoul.

Kim, K.H. 1993, *Korea—A Case of Government Led Development.,* Brookings Institute, Washington.

Kim, K.W. 1993, 'Ideology and politics of the ruling elite, both civilian and military', in *Korean Public Administration and Policy in Transition, Vol 1 Governmental Institutions and Policy Process,* eds K.W. Kim and Y.D. Jung, Jungwon Publishing Co., Seoul.

Kim, Linsu 1980, 'Stages of development of industrial technology in a LDC: a model', *Research Policy,* vol. 9, no. 3, pp. 254–77.

Kim, Linsu 1988a, 'The transfer of programmable automation technology to a rapidly developing economy: an initial assessment', *International Economic Journal,* vol. 2, no. 2, pp. 29–40.

Kim, Linsu 1988b, 'Science and technology policies for industrialization in Korea', in *Strategies for Industrial Development: Concept and Policy Issues,* ed. J. Seo, ADPC, Kuala Lumpur. (Proceedings of the conference on the same topic in Seoul on May 24–31, 1988).

Kim, Linsu 1990, 'Korea—the acquisition of technology', in *Technological Challenge in the Asia—Pacific Economy,* eds H. Soesastro, and M. Pangestru, Allen and Unwin, Sydney.

Kim, Linsu and Dahlman, C. 1992, 'Technology policy for industrialisation: an integrative framework and Korea's experience', *Research Policy,* vol. 21, pp. 437–52.

Kim, Linsu and Lee, H.S. 1987, 'Patterns of technological change in a rapidly developing country: a synthesis', *Technovation,* vol. 6, no. 4, pp. 261–76.

Kim, Linsu, Lee, J.W. and Lee, J.J. 1987, 'Korea's entry into the computer industry and its acquisition of technological capability', *Technovation,* vol. 6, no. 4, pp. 277–93.

Kim, S.J. 1989, 'Crisis, regime change and development: a quantitative analysis of South Korean political transformation 1945–1987', in *A Dragon's Progress: Development Administration in Korea,* eds G.E. Caiden and B.W. Kim, Kumarian Press, Connecticut.

Kim, S.J. 1993, 'The rise of the neo-mercantile security state: state institutional change in Korea', in *Korean Public Administration and Policy in Transition, Vol 1 Governmental Institutions and Policy Process,* eds K.W. Kim and Y.D. Jung, Jungwon Publishing Co., Seoul.

Kim, W.J. 1993, 'The Korean union movement in transition', in *Organised Labor in the Asia Pacific Region: A Comparative Study of Trade Unionism in Nine Countries,* ed. S. Frankel, ILR Press, Ithaca, New York.

Kim, W.S. and Lee, K.C. 1990, *The International Dimension of Korean Tax Policy,* Korea University, Seoul.

Kim, Y.H. 1987, 'Towards an articulation of the dependency-development paradigm', in *Dependency Issues in Korean Development.,* ed. K.D. Kim, Seoul National University Press, Seoul.

Kim, Y.H. 1994, 'An introduction to the Korean model of political economy', in *Korea's Political Economy: An Institutional Perspective,* eds L.J. Cho and Y.H. Kim, Westview Press, Boulder, Colorado.

Kim, Y.R. 1992, 'Korean labour movement and political participation', *Korean Observer*, vol. 23, no. 1, pp. 1–18.

Kobrin, S.J. 1987, 'Testing the bargaining hypothesis in the manufacturing sector in developing countries', *International Organisation*, vol. 41, Autumn, pp. 609–38.

Kohli, A. 1994, 'Where do the high growth political economies come from? The Japanese lineage of Korea's "developmental state"', *World Development*, vol. 22, no. 9, pp. 1269–93.

Koo, B.H. and Bark, T. 1988, 'Recent trends, government policies and the economic impact of direct foreign investment in Korea', *FAIR Conference: The First Conference on Asia-Pacific Relations—Towards the Future of the Asia-Pacific Area*, vol. 2, Foundation for Advanced Information and Research, Tokyo.

Koo, B.Y. 1982, *New Forms of Foreign Investment in Korea*, Korea Development Institute Working Paper Series 82–02, Seoul.

Koo, B.Y. 1984, *Industrial Structure and Foreign Investment: A Case Study of their Interrelationship for Korea*, Korean Development Institute Working Paper Series 84–02, Seoul.

Koo, B.Y. 1985, 'The role of direct foreign investment in Korea's recent economic growth', in *Foreign Trade and Investment*, ed. W. Galenson, University of Wisconsin Press, Madison.

Koo, H. 1987, 'The interplay of state, social class and world system in East Asian development: the case of South Korea and Taiwan', in *The Political Economy of the New Asian Industrialism*, ed. F. Deyo, Cornell University Press, Ithaca.

Koo, H. 1990, 'From farm to factory: proletarianization in Korea', *American Sociological Review*, vol. 55, no. 5, pp. 669–79.

Koo, H. (ed) 1993, *State and Society in Contemporary Korea*, Cornell University Press, Ithaca.

Koo, H. and Kim, E.M. 1992, 'The developmental state and capital accumulation in South Korea', in *States and Development in the Asian Pacific Rim*, eds R.P. Applebaum and J. Henderson, Sage Publications, London.

Krasner, S.D. 1978, *Defending the National Interest*, Princeton University Press, Princeton, New Jersey.

Krasner, S.D. 1995, 'Power politics, institutions and transnational relations' in *Bringing Transnational Relations Back In: Non State Actors, Domestic Structures and International Institutions*, ed. T. Risse-Kappen, Cambridge University Press, Cambridge.

Krugman, P.R. 1983, 'The "new theories" of international trade and the multinational enterprise', in *The Multinational Corporation in the 1980s*, eds C.P. Kindleberger and D.B. Audretsch, The MIT Press, Cambridge, Massachusetts.

Kuznets, P. 1994, *Korean Economic Development: An Interpretative Model*, Greenwood Publishing, Westport, Connecticut.

Kwon, J. 1994, 'The East Asia challenge to neoclassical orthodoxy', *World Development*, vol. 22, no. 4, pp. 635–44.

Lall, S. 1992, 'Technological capabilities and industrialisation', *World Development*, vol. 20, no. 2, pp. 165–86.

Lall, S. 1994, 'The East Asian miracle: does the bell toll for industrial strategy?', *World Development*, vol. 22, no. 4, pp. 645–54.

Lall, S. and Streeten, P. 1977, *Investment, TNCs and Developing Countries*, Macmillan, London.

Launius, M.A. 1984, 'The state and industrial labor in South Korea', *Bulletin of Concerned Asian Scholars*, vol. 16, no. 4, pp. 2–10.

Lee, C.H. 1980, 'United States and Japanese direct investment in Korea: a comparative study', *Hitotsubashi Journal of Economics*, February, pp. 26–41.

Lee, C.H. 1984, 'Transfer of technology from Japan and the United States to Korean manufacturing industries: a comparative study', *Hitisubashi Journal of Economics,* vol. 25, pp. 125–36.

Lee, C.H. 1992, 'The government, financial system, and large private enterprises in the economic development of South Korea', *World Development*, vol. 20, no. 2, pp. 187–97.

Lee, H.K. 1994, *Foreign Direct Investment and Policy in Korea*, Korea Development Institute, Seoul (in Korean).

Lee, K. and Lee, C.H. 1992, 'Sustaining economic development in South Korea: lessons from Japan', *The Pacific Review,* vol. 5, no. 1, pp. 13–24.

Lee, K.U. 1986, *Industrial Development: Policies and Issues,* Korea Development Institute, Seoul.

Lee, M.W. 1990, *The Odyssey of Korean Democracy: Korean Politics, 1987– 1990*, Praeger, New York.

Lee, M.W. 1995, 'South Korea's politics of succession and the December 1992 presidential election', in *Politics and Policy in the New Korean State*, ed. J. Cotton, Longman Australia, Melbourne.

Lee, S.C. 1995, 'Deregulation policy in Korea', in *Privatization and Deregulation: The International Experience and Korea's Approach*, eds S.C. Lee, and J.H. Kim, Korea Economic Research Institute, Seoul.

Lee, W.Y. 1989, 'Role of small and medium sized enterprises of industrialized countries in the transfer of technology to the Republic of Korea', *Asian Economies*, no. 69, pp. 40–69.

Lee, W.Y. 1987, *Direct Foreign Investment in Korea: Pattern, Impacts, and Government Policy,* 'Korea Development Institute Working Paper No. 87–06, Seoul.

Liddle, R.W. 1992, 'The politics of development policy', *World Development*, vol. 20, no. 6, pp. 793–807.

Lie, J. 1991, 'The prospect for economic democracy in South Korea', *Economic and Industrial Democracy*, vol. 12, pp. 501–13.

Lim, D. 1983, 'Fiscal incentives and direct foreign investment in less developed countries', *Journal of Development Studies*, vol. 19, no. 2, pp. 207–12.

Lim, D. 1994, 'Explaining the Growth Performances of Asian developing economies', *Economic Development and Cultural Change*, vol. 42, July, pp. 829–44.

Lim, H.C. and Kim, B.K. 1995, *Corporatism revisited: labour movement and democratizaton in Korea*, Korea University.

Lim, H.C. and Jong, H.Y. 1987, ' The state, local capitalists and multinationals: the changing nature of a triple alliance in Korea', *Dependency Issues in Korean Development*, ed. K. D. Kim, Seoul National University Press, Seoul.

Lizondo, J.S. 1991, 'Foreign direct investment', in *Determinants and Systemic Consequences of International Capital Flows*, International Monetary Fund Occasional Paper 77, Washington.

Luedde-Neurath, R. 1984, 'State intervention and foreign direct investment in South Korea', *IDS Bulletin*, vol. 15, no. 2, pp. 18–25.

Luedde-Neurath, R. 1985, 'State intervention and export oriented development in South Korea', in *Developmental States in East Asia*, ed. G. White, MacMillan Press, London.

MacIntyre, A.J. 1990, *Business Government Relations in Industrialising East Asia: South Korea and Thailand*, Australia Asia Papers No. 53, Centre for the Study of Australia Asia Relations, Griffith University, Brisbane.

MacCormack, G. and Gittings, J.G. (eds) 1977, *Crisis in Korea*, Spokesman Books, London.

Mardon, R. 1990, 'The state and the effective control of foreign capital: the case of South Korea', *World Politics,* vol. 40, October, pp. 111–38.

Mardon R. 1991, 'The state and industrial transformation in the Republic of Korea,' *Journal of Social Political and Economic Studies*, vol. 15, Winter, pp. 457–82.

Martellaro, J.A. 1991, 'Economic growth in East Asia and the Confucian ethic', *Asian Profile*, vol. 19, no. 1, pp. 81–9.

Matthews, T. and Ravenhill, J. 1994, 'Strategic trade policy: the Northeast Asian Experience, in *Business and Government in Industrialising Asia*, ed. A. MacIntrye, Allen and Unwin, Sydney.

Matsura, N.F. 1989, 'Management conflict and foreign direct investment: the case of Japanese investment in South Korea', *Columbia Journal of World Business*, Summer, pp. 61–7.

Ministry of Finance and Korea Development Bank 1993, *Korea's Foreign Capital Inducement in the Past Thirty Years,* Seoul (in Korean).

Ministry of Finance 1994a, *Reform Plans for Improvement in the Foreign Investment Environment,* Seoul.

Ministry of Finance 1994b, *The Foreign Investment System in Korea*, Seoul.

Ministry of Finance and Economy 1995a, *Foreign Direct Investment Environment Improvement Plan*, Seoul.

Ministry of Finance and Economy 1995b, *The 1995 Five Year Liberalization Plan for Foreign Direct Investment'*, Seoul.

Ministry of Finance and Economy 1995c, *Trends In Foreign Investment and Technology Inducement*, Seoul.

Moon, C.I. 1994, 'Changing patterns of business government relations in South Korea', in *Business and Government in Industrialising Asia*, ed. A. MacIntyre, Allen and Unwin, Sydney.

Moon, C.I. and Kim, Y.C. (forthcoming), 'A circle of paradox: development, politics and democracy in South Korea', in *Democracy and Development: Essays on Theory and Practice*, ed. A. Leftwich, Policy Press, Cambridge.

Moon, C.I and Prasad, R. 1994, ' Beyond the developmental state: networks, politics, and institutions', *Governance*, vol. 7, no. 4. pp. 360–86.

Moran, T.H. 1978, 'Multinational corporations and dependency: a dialogue for dependistas and nondependistas', in *American Multinational and American Interests*, eds C.F. Bergsten, T.O. Horst and T.H. Moran, The Brookings Institute, Washington.

Moran, T.H. (ed) 1985, *Multinational Corporations: The Political Economy of Foreign Direct Investments*, Lexington Books, Lexington, Massachusetts.

Moran, T.H. 1991, 'Shaping a future for foreign direct investment in the Third World', in *Foreign Direct Investments*, eds H.W. Singer, N. Hatti and R. Tandon, Indus Publishing Company, New Delhi.

Muramatsu, M. 1993, 'Patterned pluralism under challenge: the policies of the 1980s', in *Political Dynamics in Contemporary Japan*, eds G.D. Allinson and Y. Sone, Cornell University Press, Ithaca.

Nam, H.C. 1993, *A Life Story of President Kim Young-sam*, Bansok Publishing Company, Seoul.

Nam, S.W. 1991, *The Korean Economy at a Crossroads: Recent Policy Efforts and New Challenges*, Korean Development Institute Working Paper No. 9124, Seoul.

Naya, S. and Ramstetter, E.D. 1988, 'Policy interactions and direct foreign investment in East and Southeast Asia', *Journal of World Trade*, pp. 57–71.

Newfarmer, R.S. 1983, 'Multinationals and marketplace magic in the 1980s', in *The Multinational Corporation in the 1980s*, eds C.P. Kindleberger and D.B. Audretsch, The MIT Press, Cambridge, Massachusetts.

Noland, M. 1992, *The Origins of U.S.—Korea Trade Frictions*, Korea Development Institute Working Paper No. 9203, Seoul.

OECD 1983, *Investing in Developing Countries*, OECD, Paris.

OECD 1989, *Investment Incentives and Disincentives: Effects on International Direct Investment*, OECD, Paris.

OECD 1993, *Promoting FDI in Developing Countries*, OECD, Paris.

Ogle, G.E. 1990, *South Korea; Dissent Within the Economic Miracle*, Zed Books Ltd, London.

Oh, J.C.H. 1994, 'The future of democracy and economic growth in Korea' *Korea Observer*, vol. 25, no. 1, pp. 47–63.

Olson, Mancur 1982, *The Rise and Decline of Nations: Economic Growth, Stagnation and Social Rigidities*, Yale University Press, New Haven.

Onis, Z. 1991, 'The logic of the developmental state', *Comparative Politics*, vol. 24, no. 1, pp. 109–26.

O'Sullivan, P. 1985, 'Determinants and impact of private foreign direct investment', *Management International Review*, vol. 25, no. 4, pp. 28–34.

Pae, S.M. 1986, *Testing Democratic Theories in Korea*, University Press of America, Lanham.

Page, J.M. 1994, 'The East Asian miracle: an introduction', *World Development*, vol. 22, no. 4, pp. 615–25.

Paik, W.K. 1991a, 'Merits and demerits of public administration in Korea's modernization', in *A Dragon's Progress: Development Administration in Korea*, eds G.E. Caiden and B.W. Kim, Kumarian Press, Connecticut.

Paik, W.K. 1991b, 'The formation of the governing elites in Korean society' in *A Dragon's Progress: Development Administration in Korea*, eds G.E. Caiden and B.W. Kim, Kumarian Press, Connecticut.

Park, C.H. 1979, *Korea Reborn: A model for Development*, Prentice Hall, Englewood Cliffs, N.J.

Park, D.W. 1993, 'An empirical study on the role of Korean administrative bureaucrats in public policy process', in *Korean Public Administration and Policy in Transition: Vol 1. Governmental Institutions and Policy Process*, eds K.W. Kim and Y.D. Jung, Jangwon Publishing Co., Seoul.

Park, E.Y. and Kim, J.H. 1992, *Foreign Direct Investment for Industrial Restructuring*, KDI Working Paper No. 9214, Korea Development Institute, Seoul.

Park, M.K. 1987, 'Interest representation in South Korea: the limits of corporatist control', *Asian Survey*, vol. 27, no. 8, pp. 903–18.

Park, S.B. 1994, *Trends and Recent Developments in the Korean Economy*, Carleton Economic Papers 94–02, Carleton University, Ottawa.

Park, T.W. 1987, 'From dependent development to dependency reversal: a theoretical and empirical examination of NIC's growth', in *Dependency Issues in Korean Development*, ed. K.D. Kim, Seoul National University Press, Seoul.

Park, W.H. 1995, 'Korea's economic diplomacy on capital and technology', in *Korea's Economic Diplomacy: Survival as a Trading Nation*, ed. The IPE Program, The Segong Institute, Seoul.

Park, Y.B. 1993, 'Industrial relations and labour law developments in the Republic of Korea', *International Labour Review*, vol. 132, no. 5–6, pp. 581–2.

Parry, T.G. 1988, 'The role of foreign capital in East Asian industrialisation, growth and development, in *Achieving Industrialisation in East Asia*, ed. H. Hughes, Cambridge University Press, Cambridge, New York.

Perkins, D.H. 1994, 'There are at least three models of East Asian development', *World Development*, vol. 22, no. 4, pp. 655–61.

Pfeffermann, G.P. 1991, 'Foreign direct investment in developing countries' in *Foreign Direct Investments*, eds H.W. Singer, N. Hatti and R. Tandon, Indus Publishing Company, New Delhi.

Pfeffermann, G.P. 1992, 'Facilitating foreign investment', *Finance and Development*, March, pp. 46–7.

Ramstetter, E.(ed) 1991, *FDI in Asia's Developing Economies and Structural Change in the Asia Pacific Region*, Westview Press, Boulder, Colorado.

Rasiah, R. 1995, *Foreign Capital and Industrialization in Malaysia*, St. Martin's Press, New York.

Reidel, J. 1988, 'Economic development in East Asia: doing what comes naturally?' in *Achieving Industrialisation in East Asia*, ed. H. Hughes, Cambridge University Press, Cambridge, New York.

Reuber, G.L.(ed) 1973, *Private Foreign Investment in Development*, Clarendon Press, Oxford.

Reuber, G.L. 1974, Some aspects of private direct investment in the developing countries, paper prepared for the South East Asia Development Advisory Group seminar on Multinational Corporations in South East Asia, Rasa Sayang Hotel, Peneng, Malaysia, June 2–26.

Rhee, J.C. 1994, *The State and Industry in South Korea: The Limits of the Authoritarian State*, Routledge, London.

Risse-Kappen, T. 1995, *Bringing Transnational Relations Bank In: Non Sate Actors, Domestic Structures and International Institutions*, Cambridge University Press, Cambridge, New York.

Ro, C.H. 1993, *Public Administration and the Korean Transformation*, Kumarian Press, Seoul.

Root, F.R. and Ahmed, A.A. 1978, 'The influence of policy instruments on manufacturing direct investments in developing countries', *Journal of International Business Studies*, vol, 9, pp. 81–93.

Root, F.R. and Ahmed, A.A. 1979, 'Empirical determinants of manufacturing direct foreign investment in developing countries', *Economic Development and Cultural Change*, vol. 27, pp. 751–67.

Rueschemeyer, D. and Evans, P.B. 1985, 'The state and economic transformation: toward an analysis of the conditions underlying effective intervention', in *Bringing the State Back In*, eds P. Evans, D. Rueschemeyer and T. Skocpol, Cambridge University Press, Cambridge, New York.

Safarian, A.E. 1972, 'Problems of host countries', in *Direct Foreign Investment*, ed. P. Drysdale, Australian National University Press, Canberra.

Sano, J.R. 1977, 'Foreign capital and investment in South Korean development', *Asian Economies,* no. 23, pp. 41–61.

Shafer, D.M. 1990, 'Sectors, states and social forces: Korea and Zambia confront economic restructuring', *Journal of Public Policy*, January, pp. 127–50.

Shaw, W. 1991, *Human Rights in Korea: Historical and Policy Perspectives*, Harvard University Press, Cambridge, Mass.

Shin, R.W. 1991, 'The role of industrial policy agents: a study of Korean intermediate organizations as a policy network', *Pacific Focus*, vol, 6, no. 2, pp. 49–64.

Shepherd, D.A., Silbertson, A. and Strange, R. 1985, *British Manufacturing Investment Overseas,* Methuen, London.

Singer, H.W. and Ansari, J.A. 1977, *Rich and Poor Countries*, Allen and Unwin, London.

Skocpol, T. 1985, 'Bringing the state back in: strategies of analysis in current research', in *Bringing the State Back In*, eds P. Evans, D. Rueschemeyer and T. Skocpol, Cambridge University Press, Cambridge, New York.

Smith, H. 1995, 'Industry policy in East Asia', *Asian Pacific Economic Literature*, vol. 9, no. 1, pp. 17–39.

Stallings, B. 1991, 'The role of foreign capital in economic development', in *Manufacturing Miracles: Paths of industrialisation in Latin America and East Asia*, eds G. Gereffi, and D.L. Wyman, Princeton University Press, New Jersey.

Stepan, A. 1978, *The State and Society: Peru in Comparative Perspective*, Princeton University Press, Princeton, New Jersey.

Stoever, W. 1982, 'Endowment, priorities, and policies: an analytical scheme for the formulation of developing country policy toward foreign investment', *Columbia Journal of World Business*, Fall, pp. 3–15.

Stoever, W. 1985, 'The stages of developing country policy toward foreign investment', *Columbia Journal of World Business,* Fall, pp. 3–11.

Stoever, W. 1986, 'Foreign investment as an aid in moving from least developed to newly industrializing: a study in Korea', *The Journal of Developing Areas*, vol. 20, pp. 223–48.

Stoever, W. 1989, 'Methodological problems in assessing developing country policy toward foreign manufacturing investment', *Management International Review*, vol. 29, no. 4, pp. 68–77.

Streeten, P. 1991, 'The role of direct private foreign investments in poor countries', in *Foreign Direct Investments*, eds H.W. Singer, N. Hatti and R. Tandon, Indus Publishing Company, New Delhi.

Sunoo, H.H. 1978, 'Economic development and foreign control in South Korea', *Journal of Contemporary Asia*, vol. 8, pp. 322–39.

The 1980s—Meeting the New Challenge: Selected Speeches of Chun Doo Hwan, Korea Textbook Co., Seoul.

Thirlwall, A.P. 1972, *Growth and Development*, Macmillan Press, London.

Tsiang, S.C. and Woo, R.I. 1985, 'Foreign trade and investment boosters for take off: The references of the four Asian newly industrializing countries', in *Foreign Trade and Investment*, ed. W. Galenson, University of Wisconsin Press, Madison.

United Nations Centre on Transnational Corporations 1991, *Government Policies and Foreign Direct Investment*, United Nations, New York.

United Nations Centre on Transnational Corporations 1992a, *The Determinants of Foreign Direct Investment: A Survey of the Evidence*, United Nations, New York.

United Nations Centre on Transnational Corporations 1992b, *World Investment Report 1992: Transnational Corporations as Engines of Growth*, United Nations, New York.

United States International Trade Commission 1989, *Foreign Barriers or Other Restrictions that Prevent Foreign Capital from Bringing the Benefits of foreign Government programs*, report to the USTR and the Congress on Investigation no. 332–268 under Section 332(8) of the Tariff Act of 1930, USITC 2212, Washington, D.C.

Vernon, R. 1966, 'International investment and international trade in the product cycle', *Quarterly Journal of Economics*, vol. 30, pp. 190–207.

Vernon, R. 1971, *Sovereignty at Bay: The Multinational Spread of U.S. Enterprises*, New York Basic Books, New York.

Vittas, D. and Cho, Y.J. 1994, 'The role of credit policies in Japan and Korea', *Finance and Development*, March, pp. 10–12.

Wade, R. 1988, 'The role of government in overcoming market failure in Taiwan, Republic of Korea and Japan', in *Achieving Industrialisation in East Asia*, ed. H. Hughes, Cambridge University Press, Cambridge, New York.

Wade, R. 1991, *Governing the Market: Economic Theory and the Role of Government in East Asian Industrialisation*, Princeton University Press, Princeton, New Jersey.

Wade, R. 1992, 'East Asia's economic success: conflicting perspectives, partial insights, shaky evidence', *World Politics*, vol. 44, pp. 270–320.

Warr, P.G. 1986, 'Korea's Masan free export zone: benefits and costs', *The Developing Economies*, pp. 169–84.

Weigand, R. 1986, 'International investments: weighing the incentives', *Harvard Business Review*, July/August, pp. 146–52.

Weigel, D.R. 1988, 'Investment in LDCs: the debate continues', *Columbia Journal of World Business*, Spring, pp. 5–9.

Weiss, L. 1994, 'Government-business relations in East Asia: the changing basis of state capacity', *Asian Perspective*, vol. 18, no. 2, pp. 85–118.

Wells, L.E. and Encarnation, D.J. 1985, 'Sovereignty en Garde: negotiating with foreign investors', *International Organisation*, vol. 39, no. 1, pp. 47–78.

Westphal, L.E. 1990, 'Industrial policy in an export propelled economy: lessons from South Korea's experience', *Journal of Economic Perspectives*, vol. 4, no. 3, pp. 41–59.

Westphal, L.E., Kim, Linsu and Dahlman, C.J. 1985, 'Reflections on Korea's acquisition of technological capacity', *International Technology Transfer: Concepts, Measures, and Comparisons*, eds N. Rosenberg and C. Frischtak, Pergamion Press, New York.

Westphal, L.E., Rhee, Y.W. and Purcell, G. 1979, 'Foreign influences on Korean industrial development', *Oxford Bulletin of Economics and Statistics*, vol. 41, no. 4, pp. 359–88.

Whang, I.J. 1991, 'Government direction of the Korean economy', in *A Dragon's Progress: Development Administration in Korea*, eds G.E. Caiden and B.W. Kim, Kumarian Press, Connecticut.

Wheeler, J. 1988, 'Problems and paradoxes: the elusive tax incentive', *Bulletin of International Fiscal Documentation*, July, pp. 319–23.

White, G, and Wade, R. 1987, 'Developmental states and markets in East Asia: an introduction', in *Developmental States in East Asia*, ed. G. White, Macmillan, London.

Wilkinson, B. 1994, 'The Korean labour problem', *British Journal of Industrial Relations*, vol. 32, no. 3, pp. 339–58.

Willis, G.F. 1985, 'Riding a tiger: Joint ventures under Korea's new foreign capital inducement act', *Journal of International Law and Politics*, vol. 17, pp. 1023–50.

Woo, J.E. 1991, *Race to the Swift: State and Finance in Korea's Industrialization*, Colombia University Press, New York.

Woo-Cumings, M. 1995, 'The Korean bureaucratic state: historical legacies and comparative perspectives', in *Politics and Policy in the New Korean State*, ed. J. Cotton, Longman Australia, Melbourne.

World Bank 1987, *World Development Report 1987*, Oxford University Press, New York.

World Bank 1993, *The East Asian Miracle: Economic Growth and Public Policy*, Oxford University Press. New York.

World Bank 1994, *East Asian Leadership in Liberalisation: A Discussion Paper on Building on the Uruguay Round*, World Bank, Washington, DC.

Yang, S.C. 1994, *The North and South Korean Political Systems: A Comparative Analysis*, Westview Press, Boulder, Colorado.

Yang, S.C. 1995, 'An analysis of South Korea's political process and party politics', in *Politics and Policy in the New Korea State*, ed. J. Cotton, Longmans Australia, Melbourne.

Yanagihara, T. 1994, 'Anything new in the Miracle report? Yes and no', *World Development*, vol. 22, no. 4, pp. 663–70.

Yang, Y. 1972, 'Foreign investment in developing countries', in *Direct Foreign Investment in Asia and the Pacific*, ed. P. Drysdale, University of Toronto Press, Toronto, Canada.

Yeom, J.H. 1994, Political economy of economic restructuring in Korea: an institutional approach to the government and business relationship, a paper prepared for the International Symposium A Comparative Study of Structural Adjustment in the Economy: Latin America and East Asia, Tsukuba Science City, November 25–7.

Yoo, J. 1989, *The Government in Korean Economic Growth*, KDI Working Paper No. 8904, Seoul.

Yoo, S.M. 1995, *Chaebol in Korea: Misceptions, Realities, and Policies*, KDI Working Paper No. 9507, Seoul.

Yoo, Y. 1982, 'Industry structure and degree of foreign ownership: a study of foreign direct investments in Korea', *The Journal of East Asian Affairs*, vol. 1, pp. 332–74.

Yoon, D.K. 1990, *Law and Political Authority in South Korea*, Westview Press, Boulder, Colorado.

Yoon, Y.O. 1991, *Korean Legislative Behaviour: A Longitudinal Analysis in Comparative Perspective*, Kookmin University Press, Seoul.

Youn, J.S. 1991, 'Korean democracy and the limits of political engineering', in *A Dragon's Progress: Development Administration in Korea*, eds G.E. Caiden and B.W. Kim, Kumarian Press, Connecticut.

Young, S.G. 1988, *Trade Policy Problems in the Republic of Korea and their Implications for Korea-U.S. Cooperation*, KDI Working Paper No. 8824, Seoul.

Yu, H.S. 1993, 'Industrial structure and labor movement: comparative study of South Korea and Taiwan' *Korea Observer*, Summer, pp. 265–90.

Zysman, J. 1994, 'Korean choices and patterns of advanced country development', in *Korea's Political Economy: An Institutional Perspective*, eds L.J. Cho and Y.H. Kim, Westview Press, Boulder, Colorado.

List of Newspapers and Magazines
Asian Business
Business Korea
East Asian Executive Reports
Economist
Far Eastern Economic Review (*FEER*)
Financial Post
Financial Times
Globe and Mail
International Business Week
Korea Economic Daily (KED)
Reuters News Service (Reuters)

Index

For Product Safety Concerns and Information please contact our EU representative GPSR@taylorandfrancis.com Taylor & Francis Verlag GmbH, Kaufingerstraße 24, 80331 München, Germany

Printed and bound by CPI Group (UK) Ltd, Croydon, CR0 4YY
08/05/2025
01864379-0001